NARRATIVES ROOTED IN TRUTH, DRIVEN BY
RESILIENCE, AND LED BY **WOMEN**.

EMPOWER HER

HANNA OLIVAS

ALONG WITH 8 INSPIRING AUTHORS

ISBN: 978-1-968061-09-8

TABLE OF CONTENTS

INTRODUCTION

A Global Shift Begins with One Voice—Then Many Narratives Rooted in Truth, Driven by Resilience, and Led by Women

Welcome to *EmpowerHER: Global Shift to Women Success*—a testament to the power of truth, the strength found in resilience, and the leadership born from lived experience.

This book is more than a collection of stories—it's a movement. Within these pages are the voices of women who refused to be broken. They've faced illness, betrayal, heartbreak, abuse, and profound loss. Yet in the face of adversity, they chose not just to survive—but to rise, rebuild, and lead.

Each narrative is rooted in truth—unfiltered and courageous. These are stories of transformation born from real pain and powered by even greater purpose. Some will shake you. Others will lift you. But all of them will remind you: resilience is not just a trait—it's a choice. And when that choice is made by women, it creates lasting change.

These women are not only survivors. They are truth-tellers, visionaries, mentors, and revolutionaries. Their stories are a powerful reminder that when women lead from experience and authenticity, they move the world forward.

To every woman who has ever felt silenced, dismissed, or overlooked— this book is your affirmation. You are seen. You are heard. And you are stronger than you think.

As you turn these pages, may you find the courage to speak your truth, the strength to rise in resilience, and the boldness to lead in your own life. The global shift is underway—and your story is a vital part of it.

Let the transformation begin.

Hanna Olivas

Founder and CEO of SHE RISES STUDIOS

https://www.linkedin.com/company/she-rises-studios/
https://www.facebook.com/sherisesstudios
https://www.instagram.com/sherisesstudios_llc/
www.SheRisesStudios.com

Author, Speaker, and Founder. Hanna was born and raised in Las Vegas, Nevada, and has paved her way to becoming one of the most influential women of 2022. Hanna is the co-founder of She Rises Studios and the founder of the Brave & Beautiful Blood Cancer Foundation. Her journey started in 2017 when she was first diagnosed with Multiple Myeloma, an incurable blood cancer. Now more than ever, her focus is to empower other women to become leaders because The Future is Female. She is currently traveling and speaking publicly to women to educate them on entrepreneurship, leadership, and owning the female power within.

Rooted in Power: The Journey to Empower Her

By Hanna Olivas

EmpowerHer

Empowerment is a powerful word that transcends mere definitions; it embodies a journey of self-discovery, resilience, and communal strength. When we talk about empowerment, we are not merely discussing the act of elevating one another; we are exploring the depths of human connection and the transformative power that comes from supporting and uplifting each other. The essence of empowerment lies in recognizing our shared experiences and understanding that together, we can create a ripple effect that enhances not only our lives but the lives of those around us. This chapter is dedicated to the exploration of what it truly means to empower her—through health, wealth, spirituality, and our very being.

The Journey of Empowerment

Empowerment begins within. It is an intimate journey of recognizing our strengths, acknowledging our weaknesses, and taking the necessary steps to grow. It is about cultivating a sense of self-worth and understanding that we have the right to thrive. In a world that often seeks to diminish our value, it is crucial to embark on a journey that affirms our identity and purpose.

The path to empowerment is not always linear. It is often paved with challenges and obstacles that test our resolve. However, these very challenges can serve as catalysts for growth. For many women, the journey of empowerment begins with the realization that we are not alone. In sharing our stories, we create a sense of community that fosters understanding and support.

Health: Empowering Our Bodies

Our health is a vital component of empowerment. It is the foundation upon which we build our lives, influencing our ability to pursue our passions and dreams. Empowering ourselves physically means taking charge of our well-being and making conscious choices that promote vitality and longevity.

Nourishment: The journey of empowerment starts with how we nourish our bodies. Eating a balanced diet rich in nutrients fuels our physical strength and mental clarity. Understanding the impact of food on our energy levels and emotional well-being is essential. Empowering ourselves to make healthier choices can be as simple as learning to cook nourishing meals, incorporating fresh fruits and vegetables into our diets, or practicing mindful eating.

Exercise: Movement is another critical aspect of physical empowerment. Engaging in regular exercise not only strengthens our bodies but also elevates our spirits. Whether it's through yoga, dancing, running, or any form of physical activity, moving our bodies allows us to connect with ourselves on a deeper level. It is an expression of self-love and respect.

Mental Health: Empowerment also extends to our mental health. Taking the time to care for our mental and emotional well-being is crucial. This can involve practices such as mindfulness, meditation, journaling, or seeking professional support. Acknowledging our feelings and addressing mental health challenges empowers us to live authentically and free from the shackles of fear and anxiety.

Community Support: Connecting with others who share similar health goals can be incredibly empowering. Whether through fitness classes, support groups, or health-focused events, building a community around our health aspirations fosters motivation and accountability. When we support one another in our health journeys, we create an environment that encourages growth and well-being.

Wealth: Empowering Our Finances

Financial empowerment is essential for cultivating independence and security. Understanding our finances allows us to make informed decisions and build a future that aligns with our goals and values.

Financial Literacy: The first step toward financial empowerment is education. Understanding the basics of budgeting, saving, and investing is crucial. There are numerous resources available, from books to online courses, that can help us improve our financial literacy.

Setting Goals: Once we have a grasp of our finances, it is important to set clear financial goals. Whether it's saving for a home, funding education, or preparing for retirement, having a roadmap gives us direction. Empowering ourselves to achieve these goals often involves creating a budget and making conscious spending choices that align with our priorities.

Investing in Ourselves: Investing in our education and personal development is another powerful way to empower our financial futures. By acquiring new skills or furthering our education, we open doors to new opportunities and increase our earning potential.

Supporting One Another: Empowerment in wealth extends beyond individual goals. By sharing resources and knowledge with others, we can uplift our communities. Whether it's through mentorship, sharing financial advice, or collaborating on projects, we create a culture of support that fosters financial empowerment for all.

Spirituality: Empowering Our Souls

Spiritual empowerment is about connecting with our inner selves and understanding our purpose. It involves exploring our beliefs, values, and the essence of who we are.

Self-Reflection: Engaging in self-reflection is crucial for spiritual growth. Taking time to meditate, journal, or simply sit in silence allows us to connect with our inner voice and understand our desires and fears. This self-awareness empowers us to live authentically and aligned with our values.

Finding Purpose: Empowerment in spirituality often involves discovering our purpose. What drives us? What brings us joy? Engaging in activities that resonate with our passions can lead us to a deeper understanding of our purpose. Whether it's volunteering, pursuing a creative outlet, or dedicating ourselves to a cause, these pursuits nourish our souls.

Connection to a Higher Power: For many, spirituality involves a connection to a higher power or a sense of something greater than oneself. This connection can provide comfort and guidance during challenging times. Engaging in practices such as prayer, meditation, or attending spiritual gatherings can deepen our relationship with the divine.

Building a Spiritual Community: Connecting with others who share our spiritual beliefs fosters a sense of belonging and support. Whether it's through religious organizations, spiritual groups, or online communities, these connections empower us to grow together and share our experiences.

Physicality: Empowering Our Presence

Empowerment extends to how we carry ourselves in the world. Our physicality—the way we present ourselves—can influence our confidence and the way we are perceived.

Self-Care: Practicing self-care is an essential aspect of empowerment. Taking time for ourselves, whether through skincare routines, pampering, or simply enjoying moments of solitude, reinforces our self-worth. When we prioritize self-care, we send a powerful message to ourselves that we are deserving of love and attention.

Confidence and Posture: The way we carry ourselves can have a profound impact on our confidence. Standing tall, maintaining eye contact, and expressing ourselves authentically allows us to embody our power. Confidence is contagious, and when we project self-assurance, we inspire those around us.

Expressing Our Style: Empowering our physicality also means embracing our unique styles and expressions. Our clothing, hair, and overall appearance can be forms of self-expression. Embracing our individuality allows us to celebrate who we are, empowering us to present our true selves to the world.

Community Support in Physicality: Just as with health and spirituality, surrounding ourselves with supportive communities can enhance our sense of empowerment in physicality. Engaging in activities like group fitness classes, fashion clubs, or beauty workshops creates an environment of encouragement and inspiration.

Connection: The Heart of Empowerment

At the core of empowerment is connection—connection to ourselves, to others, and to our communities. Building meaningful relationships fosters understanding, love, and support.

Building Authentic Relationships: Empowerment flourishes in authentic relationships. Taking the time to cultivate deep connections with friends, family, and colleagues creates a support system that encourages growth and resilience. Sharing our vulnerabilities strengthens our bonds and allows us to uplift one another.

Creating a Supportive Community: Actively participating in community initiatives and organizations fosters a sense of belonging. When we come together to support one another, we create an environment that nurtures empowerment. Whether through volunteering, attending events, or starting initiatives, engaging with our communities allows us to make a meaningful impact.

Practicing Empathy: Empathy is a powerful tool for empowerment. By actively listening and seeking to understand others' perspectives, we create a culture of compassion and support. When we show empathy, we validate each other's experiences, empowering those around us to share their stories.

Celebrating Each Other's Successes: Empowering one another means celebrating each other's successes, no matter how small. Acknowledging achievements fosters a sense of community and encourages continued growth. When we cheer for one another, we create an environment where everyone feels valued and inspired to reach new heights.

The Transformative Power of Love

Love is the driving force behind empowerment. It is through love that we cultivate understanding, acceptance, and connection.

Self-Love: The journey of empowerment begins with self-love. Acknowledging our worth and embracing our flaws allows us to show up authentically in the world. When we practice self-love, we empower ourselves to pursue our dreams without fear of judgment.

Loving Relationships: Surrounding ourselves with loving relationships is essential for empowerment. When we nurture connections with those who uplift us, we create a foundation of support that fosters growth and resilience.

Love as a Catalyst for Change: Love has the power to inspire change. When we approach challenges with love and compassion, we create solutions that benefit everyone involved. Empowering others through acts of kindness and understanding creates a ripple effect that transforms our communities.

Community Love: Building a loving community is vital for empowerment. When we come together to support one another, we create an environment where everyone can thrive. Community love fosters connection, compassion, and a shared commitment to uplifting each other.

Empower Her: A Journey of Transformation

As we continue our journey toward empowerment, it's vital to recognize the importance of community. When women come together, we create a powerful force for change, support, and growth. In every gathering—whether it's a small circle of friends, a professional networking event, or a large conference—we create a sacred space where stories can be shared, dreams can be nurtured, and collective strength can flourish.

Building Community: The Heart of Empowerment

Community is more than just a gathering of individuals; it is a support system that helps us navigate the complexities of life. It's where we find understanding and compassion, allowing us to share our struggles without fear of judgment. When we empower each other, we foster an environment where vulnerability is seen as a strength, and where healing can occur.

Consider this: each time we uplift a fellow woman, we create ripples of positive change. This empowerment can be as simple as offering a listening ear or as significant as mentoring someone through a pivotal life moment. When we support one another, we cultivate a culture of love and understanding that extends beyond ourselves.

Love as a Tool for Empowerment

Love is a powerful catalyst for empowerment. It fuels our desire to lift one another up, to celebrate successes, and to be there during hardships. When we embody love, we create an atmosphere that encourages women to pursue their passions, dreams, and goals.

Remember, love isn't merely an emotion; it's an action. We can express love through words, deeds, and the way we treat each other. Small acts of kindness—a compliment, a helping hand, or a shared resource—can have a profound impact. They remind us that we are not alone in our journeys.

As I reflect on the power of love in my life, I remember times when a simple gesture made all the difference. A friend's encouraging words during a tough time, or the warmth of a community that rallied around me during moments of doubt. These instances solidified my belief in the power of love as a transformative force.

The Role of Understanding in Empowerment

Understanding is another essential component of empowerment. It goes hand in hand with love, creating a deeper connection between individuals. To empower others, we must strive to understand their unique experiences, challenges, and aspirations. This requires active listening and an open heart.

When we take the time to understand one another, we create bridges instead of barriers. We recognize that our differences make us stronger, as they enrich our perspectives and deepen our insights. Through understanding, we foster inclusivity, ensuring that every voice is heard and valued.

Each woman's journey is distinct, shaped by her own experiences, background, and aspirations. By embracing our differences, we can learn from one another and grow together. We empower ourselves and others when we celebrate diversity and advocate for equity.

Connection: The Thread That Weaves Us Together

Connection is the thread that weaves the fabric of empowerment. When we connect with one another, we share our journeys, our victories, and our vulnerabilities. These connections create a sense of belonging, reminding us that we are not alone in our struggles.

In moments of triumph and in times of difficulty, connections can ground us. They remind us that we have a support system, that others are rooting for us, and that we can always lean on each other.

Think of a time when you felt truly connected to someone. Perhaps it was during a shared experience or a moment of honesty. Those connections are invaluable; they serve as reminders of the strength and beauty that exist within our communities.

Empowering Ourselves: A Call to Action

While empowering others is crucial, we must also focus on empowering ourselves. Self-empowerment is about recognizing our worth, embracing our strengths, and acknowledging our potential. It's about taking ownership of our lives and making choices that align with our values and aspirations.

Empowering ourselves begins with self-awareness. It involves reflecting on our beliefs, understanding our fears, and identifying the passions that ignite our souls. This self-awareness acts as a compass, guiding us toward decisions that resonate with our true selves.

Additionally, we can empower ourselves through continuous learning and personal growth. Knowledge is a powerful tool that enables us to navigate the complexities of life with confidence. Whether it's through formal education, reading, or engaging in new experiences, the pursuit of knowledge enhances our understanding of ourselves and the world around us.

Health and Well-Being: The Foundation of Empowerment

Empowerment also extends to our health and well-being. When we prioritize our physical, mental, and emotional health, we create a solid foundation for personal growth and empowerment.

Taking care of our bodies through exercise, proper nutrition, and self-care practices is essential. It allows us to feel our best, both physically and mentally. When we prioritize our health, we become better equipped to tackle challenges, support others, and pursue our passions.

Mental and emotional well-being are equally important. Engaging in practices that promote mindfulness, self-reflection, and emotional resilience can have a profound impact on our overall quality of life. Seeking therapy or counseling, practicing meditation, or simply taking time for self-care can help us navigate life's ups and downs with grace and strength.

The Journey of Empowerment: A Lifelong Process

Empowerment is not a destination; it's a journey. It requires ongoing commitment, introspection, and a willingness to grow. We must continuously strive to uplift ourselves and those around us, understanding that the journey is as valuable as the destination.

Throughout this journey, we will face challenges and obstacles. However, it is through these experiences that we find our strength and resilience. We learn to rise above adversity and emerge even stronger. Each challenge is an opportunity for growth, a chance to redefine ourselves and our aspirations.

As we embrace our journeys of empowerment, let us remember that we are all connected. Our individual stories weave together to create a rich tapestry of shared experiences, strength, and love. By empowering ourselves and each other, we contribute to a larger movement that uplifts women everywhere.

The Power of Empowerment

In closing, I invite you to embrace the journey of empowerment. Let us support one another through love, understanding, and connection. As we rise together, we can create a world where every woman feels empowered to live authentically and unapologetically.

Empower her through community, love, and understanding. Empower her through the recognition of her worth and the celebration of her journey. Empower her through the choices she makes and the strength she embodies.

Together, we can create a legacy of empowerment that resonates for generations to come. Let us continue to uplift, inspire, and transform—because when one woman rises, we all rise.

Helen Kagan

Kagan Paradigm
Healer Artist Designer President

https://www.linkedin.com/in/healer
https://www.facebook.com/helenkagan
https://www.instagram.com/helenkaganarts/
www.HelenKagan.com
www.WearableHealingArts.com

Helen Kagan Ph.D, a scientist, psychologist, healer, writer, artist, a pioneer creating art with intention to heal, is a creator of unique HealingArts™ for 30 years. As a severe PTSD survivor dedicated her life to helping others, she synergistically integrates Fine Art, Expressive Arts & Art of Healing. Her "HealingArts" shown in multiple Galleries, Catalogs, Countries won awards, named "Collectible Artist". Helen, a bestselling Author with 3 books, has her column in 2 International Magazines, was interviewed and published in many others. Dr. Kagan was awarded and published via Passion Vista International as one of 40 Women-Leaders world-wide (2023), nominated to be the Cover with 6pg Article in International Collectors' ArtGuide (2024), and a Cover with 10pg article Top 5 leaders in Magnate View Business Magazine (2025). Helen believes in art being catalyst for healing individuals & society, and in engaging Healthcare & Hospitality to encourage healing through art.

A Journey to YourSelf: Creating a Healer Within, Embodying Love, Light & Gratitude

By Helen Kagan

My chapter is dedicated to all women to acknowledge our beauty and inner strength, even when it feels like we're totally out of control or falling apart. To empower ourselves and embrace the Love and Light we're bringing to others, yet still need to learn to give to ourselves... To continue bringing our Beauty, Authenticity, Gratitude, and Leadership to the world. I am dedicating my chapter to women in every corner of our planet Earth, young and old, big and small, healthy and ill, mothers, daughters, wives, women of all races, colors, and nationalities, living anywhere and everywhere in the world, all wonderful, colorful, beautiful, powerful, vulnerable, strong, sensitive amazing women that we can't live without, women who gift the world the most precious thing – our LIFE.

I'm sharing with you my compelling stories, both heartbreaking and soulwarming. Why? Because my HigherSelf is pushing me to do so. She's dragging me to share my pains and joys, gifts and sorrows, my creative Spirit, and proverbial "lessons." I've had so many it'll be enough for thousands! (If they'd want to learn from mine rather than making their own "mistakes"... :))

Being a Healing Artist, a pioneer in creating art with the intention to heal, and a creator of my unique HealingArts™ concept, brand, and venue, I believe in Art as a catalyst for healing individuals, society, and the environment. I am a *Creative* – it's not only WHAT I do, it is WHO I am. It is my identity. And if I don't create, I feel like a fish out of water, like I'm dying. Literally. I must create, any time, any place, anything – which allows self-expression, newness, and the release of challenging situations, thoughts, and feelings. It decreases emotional response/reaction to undesirable events and stress(!) and has multiple applications for creativity. I hope most readers can relate to this, right? We, women, are very intuitive creatures (for the most part), and it's in our blood to be creative, feeling things before they happen, becoming ongoing caretakers, home-keepers, giving everything we can (and more) to our families and loved ones, while not taking proper care of ourselves until it can be too late... Loving others more than we pay attention to our own needs... Can you relate?

I think almost everyone at this point in their lives asked themselves those big existential questions like WHO AM I? WHY am I here? WHAT am I here for? What's my VISION, MISSION, PURPOSE? I find answers in basic spiritual principles (regardless of any religious beliefs): *Learning Forgiveness. Knowing your Strength. Speaking your Truth. Embracing Self-Love. Practicing Gratitude.*

I personally don't believe in "mistakes." I believe there are "lessons" given to us to learn and define our WHYs. I am finally clear about mine. I've chosen to be the Artist that I was born to be, and it's my truth. But... It took me almost 30 years to realize that this is not only a way to express myself, but to heal myself and others because this is WHO I AM! I am here to bring this message to the world that my art is truly healing, emanating Love and Light, a healing tool on your journey to YourSelf.

> Beautiful Women, we are so much to behold
> Love, Peace, and Strength we effortlessly unfold
> Caregivers, we're tender, loving, and healing
> With our Hearts and Souls, generously revealing.

> We are Mothers, we endlessly nurture and protect
> Our children, whose love or hate we can never reject.
> We are Daughters, embodying youth and grace
> Our beauty and charm, we gently embrace.
> We are passionate Lovers, we adore and ignite
> our tenderness, desire, our longing delight.

We are leaders and followers, we are big and small
We are powerful and vulnerable, but we always stand tall.
We keep our face regardless of why, what, and how
Even with a stroke of misfortune or challenging call
We are always available, we are Here and Now
With our Love and Faith, we strongly enthrall.

But... in shadows deep, where eyes can't see,
There live Beautiful Women who long to be free.
Their scars, unseen, are deep under the skin,
They bear the weight of pain and sin.

Abused, disrespected, vulnerable and weak
They're longing for love but dare not speak.
Their hearts are shattered, their souls in pain,
But yet, they strive to rise from ashes again.
For years they've suffered, silenced and still,
And bruises on hearts were put against their will.
Their cries are unheard, their grief is unseen,
They're locked in fear, they live for a dream
That someone will come and set them free
For they are precious, and they are strong,
And they deserve to be treated with love all along.

For struggling women who suffer in silence,
We must be their voice and bring them defiance.
We have to stand up for their rights and dreams
And give them hope for sunshine and evergreens.

Beautiful Women. Our Sisterhood. In the splendor
Of our generous Spirit and Soul, one shall remember
We are Divine Beams of Love and Light
We bring to others, eternal and bright.

Embracing Love, Light & Gratitude in our post-pandemic "new normal"

What is it – "new normal"? Why does it have to be so different? I am still trying to figure it out… I do know that we went through highly transformational years of many losses and "lessons," and many of us who survived, had to change our perception of what constitutes health, trust, stability, comfort, job satisfaction, relationships, and even parts of our identity, to fit in a "new normal"… Is that right?

I, too, lost many close people, friends, businesses, relationships, and of course, lots of art-related opportunities. When I lost my 3 very big, already scheduled, sponsored, curated SOLO "One Woman Show" Exhibitions (100 artworks each) in 3 major cities – Orlando, FL, NYC, and Rome (Italy), I was crushed – depressed – devastated. Many important things like relationships, dreams for the future, trust, and loyalty, became questionable too… Everything felt hopeless. And many people did not make it. But, I was alive and relatively kicking. This was most important to a severe-complex PTSD survivor who had experienced "life & death" scenarios before. As a refugee who's supposedly learned how to survive, this became another opportunity to "sharpen my skills," too. As a result of listening to my HigherSelf, daily practicing Gratitude for little things (see my Column in Brainz Magazine), and continuing to create my HealingArts™, I got myself invited to a few Podcasts, created, developed, and ran my own Virtual Solo Show, invented my new unique venue – Wearable HealingArts®, which took many years to conceptualize, bring to life, and even got a Registered Trademark. That was a real-life example of "when one door closes, another opens." We just have to be authentic, trust everything happens FOR us and not TO us, believe in our Mission and Vision, keep Integrity, and practice Gratitude.

I feel it's very important for a visionary artist to communicate a unique, strong message with our craft. A message that touches people's souls, uplifts their spirits, and warms their hearts. A message so compelling that people will want to have our special piece of art in their space and will keep coming back to it to meditate, recharge, relax, find your strength, get inspiration, love, and gratitude, and perhaps – *find YourSelf*? To experience some magic when they look at your art, and not only because it is beautiful and unique, but because it directly or subliminally speaks to your Heart and Soul. Because it is saturated with Love and Gratitude communicated through colorful vibrations, sacred geometry, and embedded spiritual messages. This is the Purpose and Mission of my HealingArts™.

But my own Journey to this deep, profound understanding was not linear, to say the least. Growing up in a Communist State of what then was the USSR, where oppression and control were a daily reality, formed my beliefs, values, and a great respect for freedom to express yourself. In 1991, I immigrated to the USA, where I brought my Jewish heritage, 3 graduate degrees, 0 English, $100, 2 small suitcases, and an unending thirst to explore the World and its meaning. Coming from a family of scientists, I was always fascinated by the left/right brain relationship, which led me to study many things – from mathematics and science to psychology, therapy, and healing to fine art, and finally create my unique concept and venue, HealingArts™. As a refugee from Russia, my art reflects an existential view of life, a desire to bridge Realities and heal the Past. The further I go on my Journey and the more I evolve, the more my art ascends to higher vibrations and reflects higher dimensions of being. Communicating on subliminal levels, it delivers Love and Healing through positively charged intention, healing frequencies of color, embedded spiritual messages, and energetically balanced composition, which facilitates your healing Journey and brings you in touch with your own Quest.

As a woman leader, what was the biggest challenge in your career?

I'm often asked this question. Can you think of your own challenges? I find it difficult to find the right answer as there were so many challenges, tests, and quests, not only in my career but in my life in general... Trying to find MySelf (which was completely lost when I immigrated to the USA 33 years ago), building my new identity in a totally new, unfamiliar society, and learning a new language "on a job," which had to be sufficient enough to speak and write coherently to "deliver my important message," constantly hitting different walls due to my immigrant status (legal), building Behavioral Health Clinics to serve immigrants from scratch, on a shoestring budget, with my broken English, getting rejection after rejection, writing RFPs, serving clients in a basement of a Substance Abuse Residential facility (which later became a favorite place for all...), dealing with unfamiliar organizational structures and bureaucracy, banging my head against many walls trying to bring my "healing message" across...

If you remember, the concept of "healing" was not so popular 30-plus years ago. Yoga was something "only crazy or hip" people do, "energy healing" sounded like propaganda, and to be honest with you, only my determination, knowledge, drive, and Faith in "I can do it no matter what!" were often my only allies. Inventing and developing from scratch my HealingArts™ business was not all roses either... "What is that? Really? How can you heal me? Holistic Psychotherapist – what an oxymoron! Who does this? What healing? So, will this painting heal me? How? HealingArts™ is something Asian, like Taekwondo, right?" And more and more rejections... Everywhere. But I think this is a proverbial "cross" we, Leaders, must carry as we create something *new* and *valuable,* and *inspire* others to follow – for better future, health, happiness, abundance. We must believe in our Dreams, Mission, and Purpose, and only then can we ignite and engage others to believe, share, and follow. The price we pay and the honor we're granted as Leaders to have a Mission and live on Purpose.

Following Your Dreams. Living on Purpose

I created my brand HealingArts™ 30 years ago when I was first practicing healing as a holistic practitioner. Being a scientist, psychologist, therapist, and counselor helped me to conceptualize and further develop my concept of HealingArts™, while being a healer and artist added beautiful ways that warm your Heart, uplift your Spirit, and touch your Soul. For 30 years, my HealingArts™ has been a one-person enterprise, which, of course, brings a lot of challenges. In the 90s, I started to develop my concept while working as a therapist, social worker, and energy healer providing services to various populations in need. At that time, I was very motivated, dedicated, and devoted to building culturally competent Mental Health & Substance Abuse Clinics for the disenfranchised immigrant client populations. I did develop and run (literally from scratch, with my "broken English", and almost zero resources available) several clinical programs for immigrant families in NYC. I was working three jobs, I had international delegations visiting my programs, my Project H.E.L.P. was articled on the front page of the *NYTimes* (1999), I had also developed my energy healing private practice basically by "word of mouth," I was using Art therapy, Movement therapy, multiple energy healing modalities in my practice, I had also enrolled myself in an esoteric IM School of Healing Arts with a very demanding schedule and profound inner work one had to embark on their Journey, I was helping people heal in so many different and creative ways, I called myself a "holistic psychotherapist" (which sounded quite provocative 25 years ago!), my practice HealingArts™ was blossoming, serving people in need of healing, and I was really happy working 25/8...

Then, I burned out. When I was picked up by ambulance from the streets in Manhattan because I collapsed due to a massive panic attack mimicking a heart attack, and spent a couple of days in the ER, I realized I had to seriously change because something was not working. I discovered my multiple former traumas got reactivated from multiple stresses I put on myself. I became a "vegetable," learning to do many basic things from scratch... I had to stop working. I had to give up my beautiful small private office in the middle of Manhattan (something I had dreamt of having for a long time). I had to transfer all my clients to other practitioners. I felt totally crushed. Devastated. I didn't know how to be sick.

But I knew I had to do something – anything, everything – to get back to "normal," whatever it meant. I had to bring myself back. I began to use every healing modality I knew, to help myself get out of that debilitating state filled with overbearing anxiety, panic, hopelessness, depression, uncertainty, flashbacks, and all other wonderful PTSD-related things... In the cold winter of 2005, I felt a strong desire, a need, to start painting. I've always painted some, here and there, but never done it consistently – I just never had time for doing art, between all my studying, degrees, jobs, and "making it in America"! I've always been too busy with my schools, jobs, family, immigration, patients, clients, projects – all of those very important things (as I thought) that constituted Life.

That was a big *Lesson*. Starting painting felt like a sip of fresh air, like a refuge, like "coming home to myself." I guess it was Divine Guidance, I was immensely grateful and felt I had to create more and more healing work – first, for my own healing as a person suffering from C-PTSD, learning firsthand that art heals! Since then, I've been developing my unique "healing through art" modality. I felt this was my new way of being a holistic practitioner serving people in need – I was becoming a *healing artist*. I felt I could serve many more people this way. Since then, I've been painting non-stop, being an f/t artist for over 15 years, and working hard to ensure my HealingArts™ has a substantial online presence, and is communicated consistently to galleries, curators, collectors, art venues and organizations, hospitals, medical centers, corporate venues and facilities, hotels, and other audiences, as I believe my unique special craft has a big future.

Are we making the same mistakes? Are they a "necessary evil" on our Journey?

I don't believe in "mistakes" :) I believe there are "*lessons*" given to us to learn from. Sometimes, they can be really hard, even harsh, but... At the end, they all appeared in our reality for one and only reason – to make us better, to evolve. I can say I made a lot of "mistakes," and not only when I first started... I always trusted people and thought that everyone I met on my Journey had the same set of values, dignity, and integrity as mine. Wrong assumption. They did not. I had people who took advantage of me, used, abused, and betrayed me. All of this is true – but only from my perspective. Because I can choose to see that "*I was given many Lessons to learn about people*," about right and wrong (for me), how to act/react, what to expect, what to do when you live your life on Purpose while they aren't, and so on. I trust that my many sad "stories" are not mistakes, but are my "old stories/beliefs," which need to shift because they constitute my "old reality," which needs to change. Do you know why? Because it helps to start anew, to connect with your TrueSelf, to live from Love and Gratitude, to embody the Light that I AM. Because I believe that "*we create our own Reality.*"

I believe life is not happening TO us, it's happening FOR us. Our experiences, both, good and bad, are given for us to learn, improve, and, ultimately, evolve. I believe these "Lessons" are given for us to shift from our "old stories" and create new ones. What is the ultimate Lesson in Life? Is it different for everyone, or is it the same for all of us, "Spiritual Beings on a Human Journey"? What is the grandest Lesson a person can discover on their Journey called Life? I believe it's when we realize (become aware, discover, have a life-changing experience/epiphany) that we ARE Spiritual Beings on a Human Journey. That we are *Soul in a Body with Mind*, and not the other way around.

It is a known fact that **Love** and **Gratitude** have the highest vibrational frequencies. When we operate from Love and live in Gratitude truthfully from the heart, we begin to live happily "for no reason," and good things begin to happen. Not because, in accordance with the Law of Attraction, everything we want magically comes to us, but because, operating from higher frequencies, we embody Love and Gratitude, and thus we become it.

I learned that for many of us, creatives, art is a spiritual path, a transformational process, a way of being. As a person who practices inter-connected mind-body-spirit, I believe that now, more than ever, our world needs positive energy and spiritually-based intentions, beliefs, and values. My HealingArts™ can be an answer for many. You can just look at my artworks, take a deep breath, inhale the bright healing colors, positively charged high-dimensional frequencies of Love and Light, relax, let go, become grateful for this moment of "here and now," and enjoy this feeling... Then, repeat. :)

Seven "Little Wisdoms" for Your Healing Journey to Well-Being

1) Identify your limiting beliefs and get rid of them

Living on Purpose and bringing my Visions into reality has always been important as I consider myself a spiritual person of integrity. Often, I find myself being conflicted by things I don't accept as "spiritual." I share my struggle as an example, you need to identify your own limitations on your way to success. Important: find your limiting beliefs, recognize areas of challenge, work on them, and hopefully, get rid of them! I've always had a conflict with how I can simultaneously be spiritual and prosperous. I thought – if I am on my Spiritual Journey, it's impossible to become wealthy. Abundant – yes! But prosperous? This is where my biggest limiting beliefs/blocks are. I've worked plenty to get rid of my limiting beliefs about wealth and prosperity, as well as on other challenges that keep me from being happy and abundant. I can't say I am where I want to be, but I know I am on my way there! It was surprising to learn that those "financial blocks" I have are indeed multigenerational and are related to my self-worth... Interesting! I know it'll be helpful for you to identify and get rid of yours, too.

2) Learn self-love is not selfishness (put your own oxygen mask first!)

I had to learn to become my #1 priority in order to show up for the people I help and assist. My "lifestyle choices" are now shifting in the direction of "what are the most loving things I can do for myself so I can help others who need me, who I am here to serve." Yes, it feels a bit weird, as I'm absolutely not used to being the #1 priority for myself. It's a learning curve, but a very necessary one, as many of us, especially women caregivers, are used to serving others while forgetting to take care/attend to our own needs.

I feel that NOW is a critical time for many of us to shift. From Fear – to Love, from surviving – to thriving, from despair – to happiness. Regardless of the circumstances. My HealingArts™ is the foundation for my own shift to Love and Gratitude. It can assist you as well, as it's based on holistic healing spiritual energetic principles embedded in each artwork.

3) Create your daily routines.

No matter what your professional occupation or personal lifestyle is. "Morning routine" is an amazing healing tool that grounds you and sets the stage to maintain the high-vibrational frequencies for the day. Meditation, breathing exercises, singing loud (a very good tool!), yoga, Qi-Gong, journaling, writing, playing music, writing "morning pages" (Julia Cameron "Artist's Way"), brisk walking, dancing, jogging, moving your body and energy needed to get unstuck – use whatever modality or a combination of that works for you. I've written hundreds and hundreds of "morning pages" while working with "Artist's Way." I choose various tools from my "healing toolbox," combining them, trusting my intuition in what feels right at the moment.

No less important is your "evening routine" – especially considering a nowadays stressful nature of our environment, jobs, lack of such, psychological and emotional difficulties in dealing with current realities, eating, resting, and sleeping disturbances, which, unfortunately, becoming our "new normal," but it's in our power to change that, too! Remember? "Change your pattern – change your Life."

4) Find what makes you happy. Express yourself!

Listening/playing music, writing poems, dancing, journaling, painting, crocheting, singing, making cakes? Get creative – just move your stuck energy and raise your vibration!

My passion is dancing, so for me, it's always the first choice to move my energy – I've been dancing every possible dance, including Shamanic Trance/Dance, Chakra dance, my favorite East Coast Swing, Lindy Hop, and others. Often, I just put my favorite music on (Big Band, Swing, Jazz), and dance by myself "like nobody's watching," to shift my energy. I usually do a combo of a few "healing tweaks" daily – some movement, meditation, deep breathing, chakra clearing, yoga and/or Qi-Gong, playing music, etc., depending on how much time I have, and other factors like – did I paint non-stop last night? Am I spending 25 hours today on creating media campaigns? Is there a family emergency? Do I have to write an article for a magazine or prepare for a show? Just be creative. Express YourSelf! Make it a daily routine. It helps a lot, trust me!

5) Remove clutter and chaos, make clarity. Stop procrastinating. Just do it!

When we are removing accumulated junk from our environment (both, external and internal), we are literally shifting ourselves from

Fear to Love. One step at a time. From Breakdown to Breakthrough. One step at a time. From Surviving to Thriving. Just one little step in this direction. Then another one, and another one. See? You are moving in the direction of your Dream Life! And we can go on and on... Remember how good it feels when you declutter your closet? Or when you clean your living room, organize your garage, get rid of stuff from your kitchen, or donate lots of unneeded clothes to Goodwill? Now imagine HOW GOOD IT WOULD FEEL if you removed all this clutter, chaos, uncertainty, anxiety, overwhelm, lack of clarity, junk, etc., from your *inner world*. It feels divine! The main thing is the notion of transformation. We are shifting our "old paradigm" – old patterns, thoughts, perceptions, limiting beliefs, reactions, and as a result, we are changing our Reality, thus – our Life. Isn't it magical?

6). Find/create time to meditate.

It's important to start doing it daily. Just try for today. Continue tomorrow. Then tell yourself that you can do it this weekend. Yes – you can do it. And then just keep doing it. You can ALWAYS find 10–15 minutes in your busy schedule to heal yourself. And... don't forget to love yourself while doing that. :)

I don't necessarily believe in affirmations. I know lots of people practice them regularly. And some are successful in achieving the results they want. For me, affirmations feel somewhat mechanical, which is not aligned synergistically with my Soul's Purpose. Affirmations feel like they're not teaching me "lessons" but rather take me away from them. I would prefer a guided soulful high vibrational sound or music *meditation, activation, or invocation,* which aligns my own energy with the Higher Purpose. A deep meditation that lovingly and carefully guides me from fear to love, from chaos to clarity, from surviving to thriving. These transformational tools need to feel "organic" with my being I want to bring in alignment with my Mission and Purpose. My HealingArts™, which I "co-create" with the

Higher Source, serves that for me.

7) Discover what you are good at. Define your Vision. Follow your Dream even if it feels impossible.

As multiple new age sources suggest – "Change your mind, change your Life." Change your thoughts, change your life. Change your attitude, perception, emotional state, your energy – change your life! I think it doesn't matter where and how you start, it's important that you start. Discover what you are really good at. What do you like? What makes your Heart sing? *Take action*. Map your direction. Listen to your *Intuition*. Follow your inner voice. Define your *Vision* in your own terms. Embrace your Journey. After all – it is your Soul Journey to YourSelf!

I keep doing it as I know it's a Process, it doesn't happen overnight... For me – it's my HealingArts™, and the many ways I can bring it to the world to heal. It's my Vision, Mission, and Purpose. But... It took me many years to get to the place where I felt certain about it, and then – I allowed myself to follow my calling despite all the challenges on the way. If I get impatient (which I do :)) – I remind myself that I am on my Quest, and the most important thing is not a destination, *but the Journey*.

I thought that if I could start a worldwide movement to bring the most amount of wellness to the most amount of people, it would be one embodying Love, Light, and Healing through the Arts. In fact, I've already started a few similar movements. When I was wearing a "therapist hat" living in NYC, I developed and ran several Mental Health & Substance Abuse Programs integrating culturally competent, advanced, and perhaps revolutionary at that time, clinical treatment, prevention, and intervention approaches. I also developed my Holistic Therapy & Energy Healing private practice, where I synergistically integrated many energy psychology and healing modalities, including Cranio-Sacral, Polarity Therapy, Reiki, EFT, Art therapy, Movement therapy, and other holistic approaches and techniques to enhance healing processes. Then, I started to create my HealingArts™, first as a healing tool for my own devastating condition (re-activated severe-complex PTSD), and then to bring healing and enhance well-being through art to everyone in need.

HealingArts™ participated in hundreds of Juried Shows and international exhibitions, always eliciting profound positive responses. Shown in many physical/online galleries, countries, magazines, and major art fairs, including SPECTRUM ArtBasel Miami, ArtPalmBeach, ArtEXPO NewYork, and Artsy.net, it won multiple awards and was just published in Contemporary Art Collectors' ArtGuide with two covers (2025). Named a "Collectible Artist" by several sources, awarded and published via PassionVista Platform among 40 Women-Leaders worldwide (2023); a Woman-Leader Cover Story by IMPAAKT International Magazine (2025), I was just offered to have my Talk Show by BoldBraveTV Studio in NYC... I am so grateful! And I feel it is my duty to continue creating art for healing. Especially, in our turbulent times, amid worldwide multiple crises, wars, fear, anxiety, stress, and uncertainty. My HealingArts™ is a high vibrational sacred space for serenity and rejuvenation, to bring healing and well-being to everyone in need. It is a Portal for intentional, meaningful connection with your True Self, to help you heal wounds on the deepest Soul level, to bring well-being, harmony, and peace. I believe in mind-body-spirit-soul, and in art as a catalyst for healing individuals, society, and the environment. As a PTSD survivor who dedicated my life to helping others, my current Mission is to develop a new unique venue integrating art, healing, fashion, and design – WearableHealingArts™ to make healing through art accessible to everyone.

* * *

I am Helen Kagan, PhD, a scientist, psychologist, healer, writer, artist, a pioneer in creating art with the intention to heal, and a creator of my unique concept, brand, and venue HealingArts™ I've been developing for 30 years. My art won multiple awards, podcasted, filmed, and shown in many countries, magazines, catalogs, physical/online galleries, shows, and exhibitions, including major international art fairs. A bestselling author of three books, including *Keys to Authenticity,* co-authored with Jack Canfield and Jim Britt's *Cracking The Rich Code*, I've been an Exec. Contributor to two international magazines with my own column, and I am working on my two new books.

Today, in the midst of worldwide crises, wars, pandemics, challenges, stress, fear, and uncertainty, I believe my Mission and Purpose is to keep creating life-affirming, soulful, colorful art to make a difference in people's lives by bringing healing and hope. I believe that now, more than ever, our World needs positive energy, spiritually based intentions, beliefs, values, and living authentically and in gratitude. My passionate, vibrant HealingArts™, called a "symphony of colors" and a "vehicle for joy and well-being," is a statement of all my beliefs. *- Dr. Kagan Creates a Harmonious World with her "HealingArts"* (PassionVista International Magazine, Cover).

www.HelenKagan.com ;
www.HelenKagan.net ;
www.WearableHealingArts.com

Adrienne Kennie

CEO of Streamline Medical Billing Solutions

https://www.linkedin.com/in/adrienne-kennie-80ab3327/
https://www.facebook.com/adrienne.kennie
https://www.instagram.com/msnikki_81/
https://www.streamlinemedicalbilling.com/

Adrienne Kennie, an Austin, Texas native, is an accomplished professional and author with a Bachelor of Science in Health Administration from Texas State University and an MBA from Concordia University. She further refined her entrepreneurial expertise through the Women's Entrepreneurship program at Cornell University. Currently, Adrienne is a Manager at a leading health insurance company. In addition to her career, she loves spending time with loved ones, traveling, crafting, writing, and embracing motherhood with her three-year-old daughter. Adrienne is a co-author of several books, including Shattering the Stigma of Single Motherhood, You Can, You Will, and Start-Up or Start Over: Just Start. Passionate about empowering others, she continues to pursue projects that inspire and uplift, reflecting her commitment to creating meaningful change in her community and beyond.

Power, Resilience, and Liberation

By Adrienne Kennie

Motherhood was always a dream of mine. Like many, I envisioned a journey filled with love and joy—the kind of experience often portrayed on television. I imagined quiet moments of rocking my baby to sleep and milestones celebrated with family and friends. What I didn't realize was the complexity of the process—the physical, emotional, and systemic challenges that come with bringing life into the world. My personal experience taught me that the road to motherhood can be fraught with complications, especially for Black women navigating a healthcare system that too often dismisses our pain, our voices, and our needs.

At 39 years old, I was pregnant for the first time. Reality set in quickly. I wasn't feeling well and took an over-the-counter pregnancy test. Even after several more tests that all read "pregnant," I still couldn't fully process the news. To make it feel real, I scheduled an appointment with my OB/GYN for official confirmation. Hearing my baby's heartbeat for the first time at six weeks was surreal, a moment of joy and disbelief. Yet it also marked the beginning of a journey filled with unexpected challenges. Due to my age, I was told my pregnancy would require frequent monitoring, which immediately shifted me into "protective mode." I was determined to do everything in my power to ensure my baby's health.

From the start, I battled extreme fatigue, which left me feeling depleted most days. I tried to push through, thinking it was just part of pregnancy. However, during one visit, my doctor diagnosed me with severe anemia. This required multiple iron transfusions, adding more appointments to an already demanding schedule. My job was intense and stressful, and balancing work, prenatal visits, and now infusions felt overwhelming. I was determined to manage it all, believing that pushing through was the only option.

The Beginning of Complications

Things became more complicated as the pregnancy progressed. One evening, I experienced sudden cramping and bleeding. Panicked, I rushed to the emergency room, where I waited for hours before being seen. After an ultrasound, I was told it was a "threatened miscarriage." Although relieved to hear my baby was okay, I left the hospital confused and scared. No one took the time to explain what a "threatened miscarriage" meant or whether I was at risk for future complications. I felt dismissed, a common experience for Black women seeking care.

In my third trimester, I began experiencing severe swelling and shortness of breath. At a routine visit, protein was found in my urine—a potential sign of preeclampsia. Despite this, my doctor dismissed the possibility because my blood pressure was within normal range. My symptoms continued to worsen. The swelling became so extreme that I could no longer wear regular shoes and had to rely on Crocs. My shortness of breath made simple tasks feel insurmountable. I convinced myself these symptoms were just part of pregnancy, unaware of how serious the situation truly was.

A Life-Threatening Delivery

Everything came to a head on October 20, 2021, during a routine weekly appointment. The nurse took my blood pressure, paused, and then said she needed to check it again in a few minutes. When the doctor entered, her expression told me something was wrong. She explained that my blood pressure was dangerously high, and I was being diagnosed with preeclampsia. I needed to be admitted to the hospital immediately.

I walked to the Labor and Delivery department in tears, overwhelmed by fear and uncertainty. Once admitted, I was given four different blood pressure medications, but none successfully brought my levels down. By 7:45 PM, the doctor informed me that labor needed to be induced immediately. Although my daughter wasn't due for another six weeks, waiting was no longer an option.

Later that evening, the situation escalated. The fetal medicine team determined that my condition was too severe for induction, and I required an emergency C-section. The NICU physician's assistant prepared me for what to expect, explaining that my baby might need resuscitation due to her premature status. Hearing those words felt like a punch to the gut. I prayed silently, hoping my baby would be okay.

At 8:49 PM, my daughter was born, weighing just 4 pounds 4 ounces. When I heard her cry, I was overcome with relief and joy. She was tiny but strong, and I knew instantly that she was a fighter. However, I wasn't able to hold her or do skin-to-skin contact. She was immediately taken to the NICU, while I remained in the operating room being stitched up.

For the next three days, I was confined to my hospital bed, hooked up to anti-seizure medication to manage my blood pressure. I couldn't eat, get out of bed, or visit my daughter. Those days were some of the most challenging of my life. I felt helpless, heartbroken, and disconnected from the experience of new motherhood. This was not the childbirth journey I had imagined.

Finally, in the early hours of October 24th, I was wheeled into the NICU to see my daughter. Holding her for the first time was a transformative moment. Despite the fear, exhaustion, and uncertainty, I felt an overwhelming sense of love and purpose.

The NICU Experience

My daughter spent two weeks in the NICU, and those days were emotionally draining. Each day was a rollercoaster of emotions as we monitored her progress. Watching her work to hit milestones—like maintaining her body temperature and feeding independently—was both inspiring and heart-wrenching. I stayed in the hospital the entire time, refusing to leave until she was discharged.

I wasn't prepared for her early arrival. I didn't have preemie clothes or diapers, and I hadn't even packed a hospital bag. My car seat wasn't installed, and I felt unprepared for this new reality. Thankfully, family support helped us navigate the challenges, ensuring we had everything we needed by the time my daughter was released.

The NICU experience gave me a newfound appreciation for the strength of parents with premature babies. The emotional toll of not knowing when your child will come home, combined with the physical and mental exhaustion of recovery, is indescribable. Yet, amidst the chaos, there were moments of triumph that reminded me of the resilience of both my daughter and myself.

Reflecting on Black Maternal Health

Looking back, I now understand the gravity of my situation. As a Black woman, I faced a maternal health crisis that could have cost me my life. Severe anemia, preeclampsia, and premature delivery are not uncommon among Black mothers, who are three times more likely to die from pregnancy-related causes than white mothers. These disparities are deeply rooted in systemic racism, implicit bias, and unequal access to quality care.

Throughout my pregnancy and delivery, I often felt dismissed or unheard. My concerns about swelling and shortness of breath were brushed off until it was nearly too late. This experience is far too common for Black women, whose pain and symptoms are frequently underestimated or ignored.

My experience has inspired me to advocate for Black maternal health awareness. Sharing my story is one way to shed light on the gaps in care and the urgent need for systemic change. Every mother deserves to be heard, supported, and treated with dignity throughout her pregnancy and postpartum journey.

The Power of Resilience

Today, my daughter is thriving. At three years old, she's hit every developmental milestone and brings joy to everyone she meets. Her resilience is a testament to the power of advocacy, community support, and determination.

Reflecting on our journey, I'm reminded of the strength it takes to navigate the challenges of motherhood—especially in the face of systemic inequities. I want my story to serve as a reminder that Black mothers deserve better. We deserve to be listened to, valued, and provided with the care we need to thrive.

Motherhood taught me that resilience and advocacy go hand in hand. By raising awareness, sharing our stories, and demanding change, we can work toward a future where Black maternal health is no longer a crisis but a celebration of power, resilience, and liberation.

Debra Hornaday

Elementary Educator and Author

https://facebook.com/debbie.dee.75

Debbie Dee is author of Moments A Guided Gratitude Journal Designed to Reveal Your Happiness. She is a contributing author of Becoming Happy: 30 Ways to Heal Your Mind, Body and Soul. She always knew she wanted to help people. Debbie Dee began working in elementary education. She claims it is one of the best opportunities she has been afforded in life. There may be a lot of gloomy moments on her job, but she is grateful to help bring positivity to her students. Debbie Dee lives a life of gratitude. She is thankful for the blessings in her life. At any moment of the day, she will not hesitate to take time to be grateful for something in her life. She believes people can change their mindset in an instant just by focusing on something positive no matter how insignificant it may seem.

The Road Less Traveled: Finding Gratitude Through Adversity

By Debra Hornaday

I thought about what to write about for this anthology. I wondered what pain I would describe here. Would it be one major event? Would it be something I experienced early in life? Would it be a recent experience most people can relate to? Would it be something related to current events?

Narrowing my decision to meet the requirements for this project, I finally made a decision. Having had many opportunities to face pain in my life, I decided to share a few of my experiences. In the end, I will have described the outcomes and the victories that transpired.

I'm going to tell you about the time I was in a car accident, describe a situation on a work assignment and share a time when I was almost taken. Hopefully, your curiosity juices are flowing. Are you ready? Here we go.

Have you ever worked the swing shift? I have. I had a job where my schedule was flexible. Sometimes I would work mornings. Sometimes I would work evenings.

During a particular shift, I was scheduled to get off at 10 p.m. I watched the clock with anticipation. In a little while, I would be checking out, hurrying to my car and heading home.

It seemed like time slowed down because of my eagerness to leave my workplace. I know that's silly. You know how it is when you anticipate something so hard, and you just seemingly can't wait for it to happen.

Ding ding ding. The clock struck 12. I'm just kidding. It was 10 p.m. on the dot, and I was no longer on duty. I walked with intention to the parking lot towards my car.

Within a few minutes, I was on the freeway heading home. There was a slight delay, as I must have blinked out for a moment. I became aware of what was happening as my car swerved. My car had just rolled off the freeway.

It landed right side up. I knew the direction of the freeway because I heard the cars passing by. I kicked my way out of my car and ran towards the noise.

Someone was there waiting for me. I think there were two people looking and waiting for me. I'm not sure. They were what I would call concerned passersby. I guess they called 911 because, at that point, I don't remember anything that happened until I was being wheeled down the corridor in a hospital.

I recall a policewoman walking towards me with a half smile on her face. I suppose she was being serious and cordial at the same time. I think she asked me some questions. She was trying to determine if I had been drinking.

The next thing you know, I was in a hospital room. There was a particular busyness about the place. However, what stands out most to me is what happened at the very end of that visit to the emergency room. It is all I remember that happened that night.

A doctor told me to move my legs. He was very assertive and unkind. If I recall correctly, I stared at him, and I didn't move my legs. You know how they say you may not remember what someone said, but you remember how they made you feel? Yeah, that one. He made me feel small, like I didn't matter.

Finally, he said you can go home. The way he spoke to me was as if I was annoying him. I'm pretty sure I never said anything to him. I guess he wanted the hospital bed for someone else. I don't know. I think it was a terrible thing, that's all I recall happening from that hospital visit.

That is where the pain began. My car was gone. It was totaled. I didn't have a backup plan. I didn't have any money. No one helped me get a car. No one gave me any money. No one offered me a ride. No one called to see how I was doing. No one followed up with me.

It feels worse now thinking and writing about the experience. I am sure I was in survival mode at the time. I didn't really have any feelings about anything that happened. I mean, I was most likely traumatized. I was afraid to drive the freeway in the rain for years. However, reliving the account so I can write about it IS painful.

I think the freeway ramp was wet. This is important because the night I rolled off the freeway, I'm pretty sure there was water on the ground. I believe that if the ground had not been wet, I would not have swerved off the freeway, even though I did pass out briefly for a moment.

I don't recall how long it took me to get back to work. I probably didn't stay home long enough to totally recuperate. When I did go back. I remember making several phone calls to people I knew who worked in close proximity to my work site. It was a chore trying to find a ride back and forth to a location that was a good 60 minutes away from my home.

One person I called did take me to work one time. I presumed she would take me back home. But when I called her on the same day to coordinate a return ride home, she had already left the area.

Another person I called, who was seemingly a nice friend, without hesitation said, "No" when I asked her for a ride. She didn't think twice about me carpooling with her. More pain with a soured friendship.

I do not know how or why my totaled car was eventually delivered to the parking lot of my residence. But while it sat there, my neighbor started selling the parts. It wasn't a secret. He told me what he did. I didn't challenge him. He was a little on the cray-cray side. Read between the lines. More pain.

Do you want to know what happened at the end of this story? Finally, I went to a dealer when my energy and my health permitted it. I purchased a car. I had been rolling for nearly three months, paying the car note with no issues.

To my surprise, one day I received a call from the dealership. They said to bring the car back. Ooh! Say what? Need I get into the details? No. But you guessed it. That was pain. More pain.

In the end, I ended up paying cash for a beater, one I drove for a long time. It was reliable, and I don't recall ever having issues with it. It carried me back and forth until I decided I wanted an upgrade.

I went back to the dealer and bought another car. It was the cutest little car ever. It was a nice color. I could ride with the top down. It was good on gas. All that. That was my ride until someone offered to buy it from me. Sure, no problem. I went back to the dealer and bought another car. No pain.

You may be wondering why I'm writing about a car accident. Why am I sharing this story? See, it represents how I have lived my life. No matter the experiences I have had, I managed to get through them.

There have been ups and downs. But through it all, through the small pain and the big pain, I have testimonies about how I made it.

I am grateful for amazing experiences, a lot of them laced with some type of pain. But without trials, I wouldn't be the person I am. Without my experiences, I wouldn't have the strength that has led me here.

I got a chance to put a lot of my experiences in a book I published in December of 2023. It is called *Moments A Guided Gratitude Journal Designed to Reveal Your Happiness*. I am grateful for that book. It helped me reflect on amazing events which occurred in my life.

This next story is one where I cringe. But the outcome I cherish. It dates back to a time I worked on a job in the public sector. Everything

I did on that job, every assignment would have an impact on my client's livelihood. I took it seriously. Let me explain.

I worked on an assignment that could be classified as an administrative law judge. I was called a "determinations interviewer." Any decision I made would determine if a client would receive a weekly unemployment check.

If their claim were denied, they wouldn't get any money. If I approved their claim, based on their testimony, they would receive their weekly checks. It may sound simple the way I'm describing it. However, it was far from that.

An example is when someone quit their job, filed a claim, and got denied weekly benefits. I mean, after all, they quit their job. When you quit your job, you would probably not be getting a check in the mail.

However, the person would have an opportunity to speak on the reason for quitting. Afterwards, the employer would receive a phone call. They could rebut what the client said. Finally, the client would receive another phone call where they could hear the employer's point of view about why the former employee quit. This would allow another opportunity for the person to make comments, hopefully, ones that would help them to be approved to receive the employment benefits.

These conversations were not held in person. There was no face-to-face contact, which meant my decision-making skills had to be on point. I was making "determinations" based on paperwork and phone interviews.

It was difficult arriving at conclusions within the time frame my supervisor stated they needed to happen. I, having a soft heart and much concern for my clients, wanted most everyone to receive the funds and benefits they were due.

That's the problem, however. A lot of these clients could not prove their case. Maybe they flat out did not qualify for the monetary compensation in question. Many questions arose, and it was tough for me to arrive at a conclusion within 30 minutes.

Yep, you read that correctly. I had approximately 30 minutes for questions, answers and a final decision. It was as if I had a person's life in the palm of my hands. That was a tough call.

One day, I decided I needed more time to work on my cases. I began going to work an hour before my start time. Also, a lot of times I stayed an hour after my official time to clock out and leave the office. I wanted the opportunity to make quality decisions, ones I would not regret.

I had empathy for my clients. I wanted them to be approved and get paid their unemployment benefits. My supervisor would tell me to just deny the claims.

They could always appeal their case. That was true. But the window of opportunity for this situation to be resolved could equate to a waiting period of two or more weeks in addition to the current two to four weeks which had already passed.

Imagine having no paycheck for many weeks due to a separation from your job. It could possibly be a total of four to five weeks, based on the details of your scenario. That's the pain my clients went through.

We're talking pain here. It was emotional for me. I, too, experienced pain. It was as if I carried the weight of my client's dilemma on my shoulders.

This would be one time in my life I could use the word "hate." I believe I hated my assignment. I pondered quitting the job altogether.

That would not be an intelligent decision. What would I do for money? How would I pay my bills? It was truly a painful situation for me.

One day, the head boss walked over to my side of the office. He stood a few feet away from my desk. He exclaimed, "Why is Debbie here?" Get Debbie out of here!"

This was truly remarkable. Out of nowhere, the office manager came to my rescue. I couldn't believe what just happened.

The next day I arrived at work, I had been assigned to another team. It was the one I was very familiar with, my previous assignment where I had most of my experience and I could probably do it with my eyes closed.

Someone was looking out for me, and I am not referring to my office manager. I am not referring to a physical being. I am talking about a Higher Power. He was the one that knew what I needed at that time in my life, and for that, I am grateful.

As I am sharing these important events that transpired in my life, I realize it is a time of reflection about the pain I experienced. But I have no regrets for what transpired in my life. And, for these experiences, I am grateful.

This next story I share is quite unique to me. It took place during my travels to another country. I remember it as if it happened recently. I would never want to be in this predicament again.

Go down memory lane with me. I was on a tour with a busload of folks. Our tour guide spoke over the intercom letting everyone know that the next day we would not be traveling together.

There would be no early morning gathering.

"Tomorrow, you will be on your own," he exclaimed. I thought about what I would do tomorrow. I mean, I didn't want to be left on my own. We were in Germany, and why would I be touring the town on my own in a foreign country?

I turned to Michelle from Pennsylvania. She had been traveling with her mom. I asked her if I could spend the day with her and her mom. She agreed. I said, "Don't forget me, OK?" Once again, she agreed.

The next morning, I arose expecting to have a great day visiting museums and having lunch with some total strangers. Well, I had known them for four days on this excursion, yet they were strangers to me.

I went to the lobby looking for mom and daughter. I called their room. I walked around the hotel, wondering where they were.

I realized they had left me. So, I tried to find someone else from my tour group. How hard could that be? There were at least forty or fifty people on this tour.

In that big lobby full of people, I saw no one that I recognized. No one looked familiar. I had to make a decision. I could relax in the hotel or wait for the city bus. I could be brave and be a solo tourist or simply chill.

I decided to make use of this vacation time, although I would be on my own all alone. I would get on the city bus, leave a trail of breadcrumbs and follow them back home before dark. That was the plan.

I crossed the street in front of the hotel, waited for the bus and hopped on as soon as it arrived. As the bus got close to the spot where I would get off, I saw a sign that advertised that it was an internet café.

Nice! I altered my plans, got off the bus and entered the building. To my surprise, I was the only customer. But it was no problem. I would just do my business and leave.

The guy in charge, who claimed he was the office manager, quickly made friends with me. Well, he tried to make friends with me. He told me I could have more computer time for free and engaged in conversation, trying to win me over on his side.

A friend of his came into the establishment. He asked me if I was hungry. Of course, I was. He said that we could go get something to eat. I asked about the location of the restaurant. He said it was nearby.

We were going to walk, so I wasn't concerned about anything. I was in good health. If anything went down, I could make a quick getaway on foot. I was brave and hungry.

We took off walking to the little pub around the corner. I met some new friends and had a good time. When we walked back to the internet cafe, I was ready to make my way back to the hotel. There was a slight situation which needed to be handled.

The manager of the internet café tried to convince me to go to his apartment and wait for him. He had some weird idea that we could be a couple.

"I'll give you a key," he said. "I'll call you a cab," he said. "You wait for me there," he said. It was unbelievable. I was speechless. I made it known I wasn't interested in this type of collaboration.

But the case wasn't closed. This guy got very assertive with me, or should I say that he was slightly aggressive? I could've easily gone into panic mode. But instead, I went into strategic mode.

I quickly became an actor. I pretended all was well. I went outside a couple of times. I looked around the area, searching up and down the street, wondering where the bus stop was. I thought about when it would arrive. I was planning my getaway.

When I found the right moment, when the manager was distracted from keeping an eye on me, I stepped back outside. I tried to change my look by putting my hooded jacket on. I turned my backpack to the front to make my silhouette appear different.

I ran down the street as if my life depended on it. I ran until I reached a space between two buildings. I stepped into this space and stayed still for a moment.

I thought the man from the café would be looking for me at that point. I was careful to stay out of sight for a moment. I decided to peek up the street where I had just come from. The guy was outside, looking up and down the street, searching for me. I stepped back into my hiding place before he saw me.

Then, it happened. I looked up and I saw the bus stop. It was almost directly in front of me across the street. All I would need to do is be on the lookout for the bus so I could go back to the hotel.

I must have waited a good twenty minutes. I kept looking up the street for the bus to arrive.

Finally, it did. I saw it in the distance about two city blocks away. I timed it so that I would run across the street at the exact time the bus would arrive at the stop to pick me up.

I was almost home free. I waited by the door for the bus driver to crank open the front door. He didn't.

After a few awkward moments, I thought maybe I should go to the back door. I was in another country, and the rules could have been different.

Maybe I was supposed to get on the bus from the back door. Hum. Everyone on the bus seemed to be staring at me while I stood outside, waving my hands. Open the door, please. Finally, a young man got up and cranked the door open for me. That was different.

No complaints. I got on the bus hoping it was the bus that would take me back to my hotel. I practically held my breath, waiting to see if we would drive a few miles down the street, make two left turns and go a short way down the road, finally reaching my hotel.

Bingo! It did. We arrived at my hotel. I gladly hopped off. I ran into the lobby while glancing up and down the foyer in search of familiar faces.

I didn't see anyone for the first couple of minutes. I took a seat in the corner of the room to reflect on my day. I thought about what had transpired that day.

I had a quiet moment to myself. I realized no one had missed me. No one knew I spent the day on my own, away from the tour group. No one knew I shed a little tear out of sadness for a family member who had passed away a year ago, almost to the exact day. No one felt my pain.

Nevertheless, I was safe, and for that I am grateful.

Dr. Tavis Taylor

PLR to Profit Academy
Positive Neuropsychology Strategist

https://www.linkedin.com/in/askdrtavis/
https://www.facebook.com/profile.php?id=100081870910603
https://www.instagram.com/digital_coaching_society/
https://tavistaylor.kartra.com/page/instagram

Dr. Tavis Taylor is a prophetic powerhouse and visionary leader at the intersection of faith, healing, and entrepreneurship. As the founder of The Great Emerge Church and creator of PLR to Profit™ and the Digital Coaching Society™, she equips purpose-driven leaders to monetize their message while honoring their mantle. With over 25 years of ministry and entrepreneurial experience, Dr. Tavis blends positive neuropsychology, inner healing, and deliverance to help others break patterns, build wealth, and walk boldly in divine identity. A published author, certified strategist, and CEO, she's trained over 500 coaches and touched thousands through her daily 5 a.m. prophetic gatherings. Her voice echoes across platforms, calling women to rise, rebuild, and reign—spiritually whole and financially free. As a mother, grandmother, and mentor, she embodies the message: "You are the brand. You are the breakthrough." Dr. Tavis Taylor is not just a leader—she is the movement.

Writing Our Own Narratives: The Courage to Be Authentically You

By Dr. Tavis Taylor

I'll never forget the day I hit rock bottom. It's burned into my memory, a moment that changed the trajectory of my life forever. I was sitting in a courtroom, staring at the consequences of my choices, and for the first time, I realized how far I had fallen. The life I had been holding together with my bare hands had completely unraveled, and I couldn't escape the reality of what my decisions had cost me.

At the time, I was a single mom to my beautiful baby boy. He was my heart, my reason for waking up every day, and the one pure thing in a life that had become tangled in bad decisions. But even his innocent little face wasn't enough to stop the downward spiral I was caught in. I had made choices that led me to serious legal trouble, and when the judge handed down the sentence, my heart broke into a thousand pieces.

I had to leave my son.

The pain of that moment is something I can't fully put into words. As they led me away, all I could think about was how I had failed him. I wasn't there to hold him when he cried or celebrate his milestones. I had let my choices take me away from the one person who needed me the most.

The shame was unbearable. I felt like the worst mother in the world. I replayed every bad decision in my mind over and over, wondering how I had let things get to this point. I blamed myself for everything, and the weight of that guilt was crushing.

But God, in His infinite mercy, has a way of meeting us in the darkest places. Psalm 40:2 says, "He lifted me out of the slimy pit, out of the mud and mire; He set my feet on a rock and gave me a firm place to stand." That is exactly what He did for me.

The Moment of Surrender

When you're stripped of everything—your freedom, your pride, your sense of self—you have two choices: give up or surrender. I chose the latter.

I remember sitting in that cold, hard place, feeling completely alone. It was one of the lowest moments of my life. I didn't have the words to pray, but I didn't need them. God heard the cries of my heart. I told Him, "I can't do this anymore. If You're real, if You're listening, I need You. I need You to show up because I can't do this on my own."

And He did.

It wasn't an instant transformation. There was no booming voice from heaven or miraculous escape from my circumstances. But in the quiet of my brokenness, I began to feel His presence. It was as if He was whispering to my heart, "I'm here. I've been here all along."

Psalm 34:18 became my anchor during that time: "The Lord is close to the brokenhearted and saves those who are crushed in spirit." I clung to that truth because it reminded me that even in my mess, God hadn't abandoned me. He was still writing my story.

The Process of Redemption

When I was released, I knew I had a long road ahead of me. I wasn't just walking out of a physical prison—I was walking out of a spiritual and emotional one, too. I had to rebuild my life from scratch, brick by brick, and it wasn't easy.

I had to face the shame of my past and the stigma that came with it. I had to work hard to regain the trust of my family and prove to myself that I was capable of change. And most importantly, I had to figure out how to forgive myself.

Forgiving yourself is one of the hardest things you'll ever do. It's one thing to believe that God has forgiven you, but it's another thing entirely to stop replaying your mistakes and beating yourself up over them. Every time I felt unworthy, God reminded me of His grace. Isaiah 1:18 says, "'Come now, let us settle the matter,' says the Lord. 'Though your sins are like scarlet, they shall be as white as snow; though they are red as crimson, they shall be like wool.'"

I had to remind myself daily that my mistakes didn't define me. My identity wasn't rooted in my failures; it was rooted in who God said I was—a redeemed daughter of the King.

Rebuilding My Life

Rebuilding my life wasn't just about providing for my son—it was about becoming the woman God created me to be. I wanted to be the kind of mother my son could look up to, someone who showed him what it meant to persevere through adversity and trust in God's plan.

I started with small steps. I found work that allowed me to support us and create some sense of stability. I surrounded myself with people who encouraged me and spoke life into me. And slowly but surely, I began to dream again.

One of the dreams I had abandoned during my darkest moments was my education. I had always believed in the power of learning and personal growth, but I didn't see how I could ever go back to school. I was a single mom, working to make ends meet, and carrying the weight of my past. But God reminded me that it wasn't too late.

Pursuing Education

With faith and determination, I enrolled in college. It wasn't easy. I was balancing work, motherhood, and school, and there were plenty of nights when I thought about giving up. But every time I felt like quitting, God reminded me of His promise in Philippians 4:13: "I can do all this through Him who gives me strength."

Eventually, I earned my undergraduate degree, and then I set my sights even higher. I decided to pursue my Ph.D. in Positive Neuropsychology because I wanted to understand how we can rewire our brains to overcome trauma, build resilience, and embrace hope. I wanted the tools to not only transform my own life but to help others do the same.

Earning my Ph.D. was one of the hardest things I've ever done, but it was also one of the most rewarding. Romans 12:2 became my guiding verse during those years: "Do not conform to the pattern of this world, but be transformed by the renewing of your mind. Then you will be able to test and approve what God's will is—His good, pleasing, and perfect will."

The Birth of Tailored Connection

While pursuing my education, I also felt a deep calling to start my own business. I wanted to create something that would not only support my family but also empower others to rebuild their lives. That's how Tailored Connection Staffing and Training was born.

Tailored Connection started as a small idea: to help men and women find meaningful work and develop the skills they needed to succeed. I knew from experience how hard it can be to start over after setbacks, and I wanted to create a bridge for others to cross into new opportunities.

At first, it was just me, working tirelessly to get the business off the ground. I handled everything—building relationships with clients, training employees, and ensuring that every person who came through our doors felt valued and empowered. But as the business grew, so did its impact.

Today, Tailored Connection Staffing and Training is more than just a business—it's a ministry. It's a place where people can find hope, healing, and a fresh start. We don't just provide jobs; we provide opportunities for transformation.

Empowering Others

Through my education and my business, I've had the privilege of helping hundreds of women rewrite their own stories. I've seen women come to me feeling broken, defeated, and hopeless. And I've watched those same women walk away with confidence, purpose, and a renewed sense of hope.

One of the most important lessons I teach is this: Your past does not define your future. 2 Corinthians 5:17 says, "Therefore, if anyone is in Christ, the new creation has come: The old has gone, the new is here!"

That truth is at the heart of everything I do. I want every woman I meet to know that her story is not over. No matter how many mistakes she's made, no matter how far she's fallen, God can redeem every part of her life.

A Message to Every Woman

If you're reading this and you're feeling stuck, ashamed, or hopeless, I want you to know this: Your story is not over.

God is in the business of redemption. He can take your pain, your mistakes, and your brokenness and turn them into something beautiful. But you have to let Him. You have to surrender your story to Him and trust that He can write a better ending than you ever could.

Jeremiah 29:11 reminds us of this truth: "'For I know the plans I have for you,' declares the Lord, 'plans to prosper you and not to harm you, plans to give you hope and a future.'"

Your past doesn't disqualify you from God's purpose. In fact, He can use your past as the very platform for your purpose. So don't be afraid to own your story. Embrace it, scars and all, and let God use it for His glory.

You have the courage within you to rise, rebuild, and live authentically. And when you do, you'll inspire others to do the same.

Stephanie Dauble

Founder of The Fullest Stories
Luxury Reinvention Strategist, Architect of Transformational Storytelling

https://www.linkedin.com/in/stephaniedauble
https://www.facebook.com/sdauble
https://www.instagram.com/daubleganger/
https://medium.com/@stephanie.dauble

Stephanie Dauble is a bestselling author, cinematic storyteller, and architect of radical reinvention. A former corporate executive turned founder of The Fullest Stories and Dreamground Collective, she rewrites the narrative of what's possible—elevating those bold enough to transmute their past into power and step into lives shaped by their most sacred self-creation. Her work serves as a rallying cry for self-sovereignty: for those who transcend adversity, rise from the ashes, and refuse to shrink. Known for a voice that is frequency-shifting, soul-stirring, and wired for limitless expansion, Stephanie explores identity, resilience, and the breathtaking power of choosing yourself—fully, audaciously, and on purpose. Through storytelling, brand alchemy, and bold mentorship, she guides visionaries in becoming who they were always meant to be. Her work not only inspires—it activates. The best stories are not just told; they are forged in fire, claimed with conviction, and lived with fearless intention.

The Sacred Shift

By Stephanie Dauble

The Reckoning: When the Mirror Cracks

There's a moment—quiet, inconvenient, unforgettable—when you realize that the life you built no longer fits. This doesn't mean that the life was wrong; it simply means you've outgrown it. Mine had been stitched together with high-functioning grit, perfectionism, and the belief that responsibility equaled worth. It got me far, but somewhere along the way, I mistook performance for purpose—and I began to feel it in my bones.

So, I paused, not out of crisis, but out of clarity. I had earned the right to know myself beyond my résumé. I allowed myself a year to sit still, not to fix, hustle, or rebrand, but to listen—to be with the parts of myself I had outpaced, outperformed, or edited for survival.

It wasn't an Eat, Pray, Love scenario. There were no passionate entanglements with unsuitable men, no handmade pasta shared with stylish expats, and no mystical gurus offering enlightenment in exchange for surrender. My healing was quieter than that—gritty, sometimes lonely, occasionally delightful, and always real.

When we commit to closing the metaphorical door on who we once were in search of the person we are becoming, we need to be relentless and unwavering. It seems to work best when we commit to a full surrender: when we shut the door behind our old self, shove our new self into the room, and no one leaves until healing is complete. When we do this, we encounter our truest selves—not just the curated parts. That's where I found her: the woman beneath the conditioning, the one who no longer needed to contort herself into a version that made others comfortable.

Looking back, I see now: I wasn't broken. I was brilliantly adaptive. Every version of me was doing her best with the tools she had. But eventually, survival isn't enough. Eventually, you want to live.

So, I stepped out of the loop—the one where I kept proving, fixing, managing, and over-giving. I allowed myself to soften. I let my soul speak. And for the first time in decades, I didn't rush to respond with strategy; I simply listened.

The Stillness: Inside the Quiet Rebuild

At first, the silence was unfamiliar. No meetings to lead. No applause to earn. No metrics to chase. Just space. And me. And then something miraculous happened: a ceasefire within. There's no parade for this moment. No fireworks. Just stillness. Breath. A growing desire to move differently in the world—not from exhaustion or obligation, but from reverence. I spent years confusing being 'good' with being whole. I didn't know that healing would demand my rebellion.

My father always said that death is like being at the deli counter—your number gets called, and that's that. I believe rebirth is the same. We can only hide behind busy careers, polished personas, and the illusion of control for so long. At some point, the soul demands its reckoning. The body slows down. The heart stiffens. The mask slips. And we're left standing in front of the mirror, asking the only question that matters: Will I choose myself this time?

It's terrifying and sacred.

What no one tells you is that becoming the woman you're meant to be requires grieving every version of yourself that once kept you safe: the people-pleaser, the fixer, the great pretender, the version who carried more than her fair share in any and every relationship and called it "love."

It is the most genuine form of loss. And the most radical kind of love.

I began to set new standards, not goals, but standards. I defined what I would allow, what I would no longer compromise on, and what I would choose, even if it felt illogical. I wrote down ten bold intentions: dreams that seemed too audacious for who I had been but felt exactly right for who I was becoming.

One of them? An uncommon vitality. Another? A love that was mutually expansive, passionate, and harmonious. Perhaps the boldest? Leaving corporate leadership on my own terms—

gracefully and powerfully—finally allowed me to dedicate my life to a purpose I had postponed for far too long. When I finished the list, I laughed, prayed, and whispered to the universe, "Okay. I'm terrified by what I just wrote... but I'm ready to play." And play she did.

The Becoming: Becoming Her Anyway

There's a unique disorientation in witnessing your dreams come to life—especially the ones you once thought were too grand, too bold, too overwhelming. I used to think my dreams were excessive. Now, I realize they were awaiting my growth into the woman capable of embracing them. Once the momentum starts, your sole responsibility is to maintain alignment. It's not about controlling or forcing things—it's about simply receiving. For women raised to strive for their worth, this experience can be both thrilling and unfamiliar.

I moved slowly, caught in the tension between "Is this real?" and "Of course, it is." I reassured the older parts of myself—especially those that flinched at ease—that nothing was being taken away. This time, I wasn't abandoning myself.

Dreams don't follow our schedules, and they seldom mirror our visions. Often, they manifest as interruptions, pain, or endings that seem like setbacks, yet they ultimately act as gateways to authentic experiences.

This statement serves as a powerful call to embrace the unknown and the divine aspects of our lives. It reminds us that by releasing the need to control every detail (the 'how'), we open the door to extraordinary experiences and transformations. When aligned with our true selves, we no longer seek external validation or permission; instead, we gain the strength to occupy spaces that once felt beyond our reach. Rather than merely striving for miracles, we cultivate an environment that naturally invites them into our lives.

This is the sacred shift.

It's not about transforming into a different person; it's about becoming who you were always meant to be—the authentic version of yourself that existed before the world encouraged you to suppress your intuition and dim your light. We were never intended to accept mere scraps of our true calling. Eventually, there arrives a point when the pull of your destiny becomes so powerful that returning to the past becomes impossible—not to the job, the relationship, or the self who believed she wasn't yet prepared. That moment? It calls for something sacred. It requires that you burn the boats.

I embraced my journey of self-discovery. I let go of my need to apologize for simply being me. I stopped waiting for others to determine my worth. And in that brave leap into the unknown—navigating the fine line between fear and freedom—I finally encountered the woman I was destined to become all along.

She was clear, soft, brave, and unbothered. She was not a new me; she was the true me.

The unknown is where all the magic lives. And the woman I am today? She was born the moment I stopped waiting to be chosen—and chose myself.

Dorothe Philippe

Dorothe Philippe
Mentor of Intuition and Telepathy

https://www.linkedin.com/in/dorothephilippe/
https://facebook.com/dorothe.philippe?locale=fr_FR
https://instagram.com/dorothe.philippe/?hl=fr
https://www.dorothephilippe.com/

Dorothe Philippe is a mentor in intuition and telepathy with more than twenty years of experience. She is German living in France, mother of four grown up children and a passionate rider since her young age. Her journey started when a healer saved her family from a tragic destiny and explained her how to tap into her intuition, an innate capacity we all possess. Dorothe then got chosen by Volcano, a young former stunt horse difficult to approach. Volcano taught her how we may become more conscious of our thoughts, emotions, actions and the language we use, so we may be aligned, succeed and lead a happy life. Dorothe works internationally as a life coach, animal psychologist and healer. She has co-authored several books and engages to share valuable information about intuition and telepathy, so that we may expand to our true potential.

Your Inner Message Counts

By Dorothe Philippe

Sluta Med Grisen

« Sluta med grisen ! » I could not understand one word of what my Swedish friend had just said to her little daughter, but I guessed what it meant. She had told me already that meals had become a crucial moment between her and her two-year-old. I looked at the little girl. Her eyes were on her mother's eyes, her little fingers in her mashed potatoes. The messy, little fingers then moved. Slowly but surely, they aimed her cheek. « Hör upp! », her mother said, which meant: "Stop it." I could understand this. The words were similar to German. The little fingers, however, slowly finished what the little girl had in her mind and then returned in the same slow manner back into her mashed potatoes. The potatoes had been in a bowl, which the little girl had reversed earlier, and which were now on the table of her highchair. I knew what would come next. You could read it in her face, and in her mother's as well. I was all too familiar with the core of the situation and the spiral it may create. I knew no Swedish, however, and the little girl understood none of the languages I spoke. So, how could I help? And with this, I had an idea. But before I continue, let me introduce myself and share some background information so that my story will make more sense.

The Power of Intuition

I am originally from Germany, but as I lost my heart to a wonderful French man, I got married and moved to France, where I am still living today. I am a mother of four, who are all grown up and living their own life by now. About twenty-three years ago, in one of the darkest and most fearful moments of my life, my entire belief system crashed, and a new world emerged, giving birth to who I am and what I know today.

At the age of two, our youngest child developed a health issue that seemed to be resistant to traditional medical treatment. Searching to remedy our child's situation, the medical staff proposed risky surgery or taking part in a trial study for a new medication. My intuition told me that none of this was safe, nor our child's solution. My husband and I turned both options down, and we got our child home, hoping to find help in Germany or somewhere else.

In sharing my worries with a friend, I then learned about a healer on the other end of the world, the Island of the Reunion. His name was Michel, and we had him come to France. Thanks to ancient healing knowledge, our child recovered completely within the few days that Michel has spent at our house. During this time, Michel also shared with me how to tap deliberately into my intuition, access telepathic information, and work with energy. You may read more about our encounter and how to make your intuition work in my chapter "Listen and Align" in the anthology *She Stands Strong. 30 Stories of Strength and Resilience*, published by She Rises Studios, as I would like to dedicate this chapter to telepathic interconnection.

Soon after having left us, Michel passed away. My teachings then continued, thanks to my horse Volcano. Difficult to touch and to approach, my horse made not only my intuition work but taught me what it means to be coherent and aligned. In the years to come, I learned Chinese medicine for horses, became a certified animal therapist and animal psychologist, an animal communicator, a healer, a life coach, and last but not least, thanks to two decades of fieldwork, a mentor in intuition and telepathy.

Telepathy And Your Other Extrasensory Senses

The word telepathy is rooted in the Greek word tele, meaning distant, and pathos or patheia, meaning feeling, perception, experience, but also affliction and suffering. Pathos is described as something that one undergoes or that happens to someone. The term was invented in 1882 by the English psychologist Frederic Myers and is defined by the Merriam-Webster dictionary as "communication from one mind to another by extrasensory mean." The Oxford Advanced Learner's Dictionary describes telepathy as "the direct communication of thoughts or feelings from one person to another without using speech, writing, or any other normal method." I believe, however, that these definitions of telepathy are only partially correct and lack important information.

Telepathy and intuition belong to what is defined as psychic capacities, or extrasensory senses (ESP). Other psychic abilities are, for example, clair-cognizance with its I-know-feeling, clear-seeing or clairvoyance with its visions, clear-hearing or clairaudience where you hear a voice, empathy where you feel the emotions of others, and clairsentience where you feel the pains of someone else.

The Innate Wisdom Within Us

Psychic abilities are difficult to prove scientifically, so they have been declared to be of paranormal nature. These faculties, however, are innate and encoded in any living being and organism, so that it may be autonomous, safe, comfortable, and thrive to its fullest.

Whilst science needs to coin terms and put things into boxes in order to allow research, nothing operates separately in nature. Everything works together for the common welfare and the much greater like Swiss clockwork. So, it should not surprise you to read that it is actually very difficult to draw a strict line between intuition and telepathy when you observe it in nature and experience it in everyday life.

To be able to access information, any living being or organism may not only count on its different extrasensory senses but also on its observation faculties, knowledge, personal and collective experience, a good dose of common sense, and its connection to what is called the

Field, this energy and intelligence which scientists admit but are unable to define and which are already mentioned by all ancient traditions. But let's keep things simple. Let us only learn about all this to then explore and experiment with everybody on our individual level.

So, intuition and telepathy happen naturally. We are born with them, and we die with them, no matter if we call upon those faculties deliberately or not. You may state that the younger we are, the more we use our telepathic and intuitive faculties without questioning them too much. We just let things happen. Growing up, our rational mind then tends to turn telepathic and intuitive information down. We may even program ourselves to such a point that it happens more and more out of our awareness. Telepathic interconnection, however, is a life principle that supports and assists us at any moment of our lives. This is why it is helpful to know and understand the following.

The Power of Your Thoughts and Emotions

Science proved that matter reacts to what we think, feel and believe. In other words, your beliefs, thoughts and emotions create states of reality. To understand this better, take a glass. Fill it half with water. The half-filled glass in itself is in a neutral state. The way in which you perceive the level of water, however, creates a state of reality as real for you, as the neutral state described before. If you look at the glass and believe it to be half full, and that there is enough to meet your needs, your observation will be accompanied by emotions like confidence, ease and trust. If you believe the glass to be half empty, and that there will not be enough water to meet your needs, your perception may create stress, unease and even fear. The water level did not change. It is still the same. Neutral. A simple state. A simple fact. Your reality, however, has become whatever you think, believe and feel. This is why quantum physics and spiritual teachings tell us to be creators.

How Your Mind Thinks In Images

Now, know that whatever you think, feel, believe, say or do is accompanied simultaneously by more or less conscious or unconscious pictures or sequences of images that you download in your mind. This comes from the fact that everything we live, observe and experience is perceived through the lens of our eyes in the same way you would record or take a snapshot with your cell phone.

The images of our experiences then are memorized in our brain and associated in virtual form or imagination the moment we have a thought or an emotion but also when we speak and act. This is why quantum physics, spiritual and religious teachings speak of us as being the observer.

In general, this automatic download of images happens out of our awareness. You may have noticed them, however, in a moment of fear or worry. We may then catch ourselves imagining the worst. In France, people still say that they "make up a film" to describe the way, in which images show up in your mind the moment you have an emotion or a thought.

Once you know that your thoughts, emotions, doings and sayings are accompanied by images or image sequences, you then will start to become more and more aware of them. This, in return, will allow you to interfere and correct your visualizations, if they do not correspond to what you really want.

How Animals Use Telepathy

Telepathy allows us to gather information at a distance. It travels over time and space, and animals use it to exchange information with other species. Animal communities are generally made up of many more members than a specific animal family, group or herd, and you may easily observe how several species live and hunt together, share food, and how they help each other. A wonderful example of this is the very ancient relationship between ravens and wolves.

Scientists stated that eighty percent of wolf hunts are accompanied by ravens, and this is why wolf and raven experts consider ravens to be the "wolf's eyes." Ravens even have their nests next to wolf caves, and their youth grow up together. Ravens make about 250 different sounds, and wolves are able to distinguish sounds that are of importance and interest to them. Wolves and ravens observe each other constantly, and behavior in one may cause an action or reaction in the other.

Telepathy, however, allows everybody to communicate and pass on information in a very efficient way as well. Let's take the example of a wounded animal. Wounded animals are not only an easier hunt for the wolves but also a quicker meal for the ravens. So, when the ravens spot wounded prey, they do not only inform each other by a special sound that the wolves recognize. They also transmit telepathic information about the animal in question and the spot of its location, thanks to what they see with their eyes.

The process of observing life through the lens of the eye is not different for animals than for us humans. In watching the scene, the ravens' eyes take in details similar to a video camera. Telepathy then allows the wolves to catch almost simultaneously what the ravens see and guides them to the prey. Animals know the geography of their territory by heart. So, it is not too difficult for the wolves to recognize the spot that the ravens transmit. At the same time, the ravens also give other details of the scene. Wolves are not the only predators around, and the ravens inform the wolves exactly about who and what awaits them, so that they may prepare themselves accordingly.

Animals are outstanding telepaths, and they use their telepathic and intuitive faculties to find food, water and shelter, to scan their environment, to know the intentions, expectations, wishes and desires of fellow species or other beings, and to warn each other in case of danger. During the tsunami tragedy in 2004, it was observed that animals retreated to safe areas in time. There are also numerous reports of domesticated animals and pets, which manifest change in behavior before earthquakes.

Gaining In Awareness

There is a chance that nature encoded mankind with similar telepathic abilities, but whilst animals still rely on telepathy consciously, naturally and without hesitation, in our modern world, most telepathic processes now happen out of our awareness. This may lead to misunderstandings not only between animals and humans but also within families, at work and in everyday life.

Your thoughts and emotions are like an invisible message sent out into your environment, influencing others and outcomes of situations, allowing or preventing you even from having success.

But how is this possible, you may ask yourself?

To better understand what is happening here, let's take the example of a family dog that used to go on its owner's bed. Now, let's imagine the dog has passed away, unfortunately, and the family has got a new dog, but now, everybody wishes to keep this dog off their beds. Fear, worries and negative experiences, however, are accompanied by more or less strong emotions, which in return go with corresponding images. In the case of our family, this means that despite the fact that they do not want the new dog in their beds, they will "see" him exactly there. The dog, in return, will scan his environment for hints and clues, how to adapt the best, and how he is expected to behave. He will call upon his telepathic abilities, and there is a chance that he will execute exactly what his new owners have in their heads.

The Power of Visualization

If you want something, your brain, or better, the Pineal Gland, which is a tiny gland the size of a pea located in the middle of your brain, creates corresponding images or holograms. Those holograms are projected like on an inner screen inside of your head behind your physical eyes. You may also perceive those images, films or visions like on an outer screen in front of your eyes or your heart.

Now, if you don't want something, or you are afraid of something, or you have a strong belief or idea, you literally see its imagined outcome exactly the same way, and it is a powerful creation in both ways. So, if the family really wants to remedy the situation and give coherent telepathic information, they must actually not spend one single thought on dogs on beds or get their picture right, which means concentrating on seeing the dog lying anywhere else.

Things go far beyond our relationship with animals, though. A study with difficult youth has shown that their behavior aligned with the thoughts, feelings and beliefs that teachers had about them. If teachers perceived their difficulties during an exam and judged them being stupid or incapable, students failed. If teachers saw their trouble but believed that they were able to succeed and encouraged them mentally, students overcame their difficulties and succeeded in their exams.

Telepathy is an innate ability in humans as well, and every single one of us is telepathically interconnected to other human beings in sending out and receiving messages. So, our actions and reactions may be influenced as well. This means without really knowing it, we have a direct or indirect impact on others and hence influence outcomes of events or situations at the same time by the way we think, feel, believe, judge, apprehend, project, trust, act, speak and so on.

Do you get the greater picture here?

Now, let's return to our little Swedish girl. Why do you think meals have become such a problem over time?

Visualization: A Tool to Create Your Reality

Visualization is a great tool to prepare animals for something new, to educate and to train them, or to transmit a message. Animal trainers have results not only thanks to their experience and knowledge but also because they are very clear on the desired outcome and visualize, more or less consciously, how to get there. Scientists could also prove that the body and human consciousness actually make no difference between physical experiences and something that is imagined over and over again. This is why top athletes use visualization to improve their performance and to prepare for contests.

In visualizing things over and over again, you program your conscious mind, allowing things to happen automatically. If done consciously, this is extremely helpful. Repetitive visualization and projections done on an unconscious level, however, may create all sorts of outcomes we do not really want. This is why catching and correcting your thoughts, beliefs and feelings and setting your inner pictures right is so powerful, and why we use positive visualization in coaching as a valuable tool. Imagining, doing and feeling "as if" are known to create desired outcomes.

It turned out that positive visualization also worked perfectly with our little Swedish girl. "I can't believe what she is doing," her mother whispered, astonished. As I could not speak to the clever toddler but wished to help the situation, I communicated telepathically, and she responded exactly to the visualization. I had imagined that she turned her bowl, took her spoon, and put her food as best as she could back into the bowl. She then finished her meal properly, grinning from one ear to the other, just like me. Her prompt reaction, however, gave me a lot to think and this is why I share this story here. Your inner message counts. It goes out, and in one way or another, reaches others.

The Hidden Power of Telepathic Messages

Years ago, I worked with a group of CEOs who had lost their job and had difficulties finding a new one despite their excellent qualifications. Some of them had gone through burnout; others had experienced situations of severe disappointment, injustice or betrayal. All of them were experts in their niche and, hence, had actually no trouble being the ideal person for the position they were applying for. In the end, however, they never got the job, with another candidate getting enrolled at their place.

Communication happens on many levels. When we interact with other people, we usually concentrate on the spoken word. We may also react to body language. We do not realize, however, the power of our inner states. How we feel and what we think or believe is sent out telepathically and is received more or less consciously or unconsciously by our environment, which may align with it accordingly.

The group of CEOs had mainly concentrated their efforts on the quality of their curriculum vitae, their presentation and pitch, but none of them had ever put their intimate thoughts and emotions into words. When we finally did this together in a coaching session, they realized that their unconscious telepathic message was fear of living a similar experience, in case they returned to work. As a result, the decisive persons of the recruiting companies felt intuitively that something was wrong and gave the impression that they were not a good fit despite all the evidence. Someone else got the job, and a vicious circle was installed. The CEOs then also trained on leaving the past and, with it, their fears and worries behind. They now only concentrated on what they really wanted, and one after the other, they got enrolled.

The Power of Focus

No matter what we live or experience, we need to be conscious that analyzing, criticizing, judging and speaking about a problem, the past or a negative event, contributes to its very existence. Once we realize this, as well as to what degree we are all interconnected and how powerful our thoughts, feelings and images are, one question should guide us constantly:

What is the outcome I really want?

World known bestselling author, coach, motivational speaker and philanthropist Tony Robbins, who helps hundreds and thousands of people to get their life back on track, states that where focus goes, energy flows. When you learn to focus your energy, he says, amazing things may happen. He is right. Let's understand further why.

Our house used to be always full of friends of my children coming over to play and, later, to study or prepare for exams. One day, a little group of study buddies of my eldest daughter had gathered to write application letters to different universities for master's degrees. As the CEOs, they all had put a lot of effort into explaining their qualifications and motivations, and in the end, everybody had their letter set up. One of my daughter's friends had even brought an envelope and stamp to post his letter right away, but I stopped him at the door.

I am a very intuitive person. I sense all types of energies and had caught the thoughts and beliefs my daughter's study buddy had about the impact the letter in his hand would make. The friend in question was older than the other comrades of my daughter, and he had studied two different subjects prior without success. I could feel his judgement about himself and how the words in his letter were accompanied telepathically by negative feelings and worries. He actually believed he was not good enough, did not have the necessary background and profile, and that his application would end up in the dustbin, anyway.

That was a very strong energy that could influence the outcome tremendously, according to my experience. "Come here," I said. "Let me explain to you what will happen when you send such an important letter in the state you are in." So, we sat again, and I explained to him how telepathy works and the negative, energetic information he had set up around his letter despite his writing efforts. We then put into words how he could see his prior experience differently and in a positive and enriching way. We focused on how he could adjust his inner state and the energy that surrounded the letter telepathically by his real motivation and what he had to offer. Weeks later, the doorbell rang, and it was him standing outside, happily waving a confirmation letter for the studies he had applied for.

Think of this the next time you send an offer, a mail or a text. Make sure your words and inner message are coherent and aligned.

The Power of Your Heart

Scientific research could prove that the heart produces a strong electromagnetic field, which goes several feet beyond our bodies. The electromagnetic field increases and decreases according to your emotions and interconnects and interacts with the field of other living beings. Science also found that the heart possesses neurons that have long-term and short-term memory and which interact directly with your brain.

Moreover, research has shown that your heart reacts emotionally to events that have not happened yet and are still in the future. For the experiment, cabled individuals were shown positive and violent images on a screen. Researchers stated that the heart is capable of perceiving the content of the images in advance, proving that our heart plays a role in intuitive and telepathic processing. The experiment also showed that it is our heart that informs the brain, which then, in return, informs the body to secret corresponding hormones, actions, reactions and emotions, and not vice versa.

Scientists then got interested in global consciousness to research in which way we are all interconnected and invented machines that are able to measure it. In evaluating the recorded data, they discovered that weeks prior to the Twin Tower attacks on September 11, 2001, a worldwide emotional peak could be observed. Researchers had no explanation for the peak until the events happened.

The Power of Doing and Feeling As If

Quantum physics explains that several dimensions exist at the same time. The different planes are separated through wave states. Depending on the wave state you tune in, different realities may be created, just like around our glass of water. Entering wave states, and how to stay in them no matter what happens around us, is something we all can learn.

During the International Peace Project in the Middle East in the early 1980s, researchers from Princeton University trained individuals not to judge and only imagine and feel peace. The trained persons were then sent into war zones during the first war between Israel and Libanon in order to see and feel peace as if it had already happened. In his conference on the Divine Matrix given in Milan on May 30, 2007, bestselling author Gregg Braden reports that the results of the experiment were so profound that they were published in December 1988 in the *Journal of Conflict Resolution in the Middle East*, no. 4, page 778. The experiment revealed that as long as the trained individuals emitted feelings of peace, peace became a reality.

Results showed that not only war and terror attacks stopped but that the numbers of crime, road accidents and emergency visits had declined at the same time. When people stopped their feelings of peace, however, statistics were reversed. The experiment was repeated over several years with always the same outcome, allowing researchers to determine how many people it needed to create peace.

According to Princeton University, it takes only a very small number of us to reverse things: 100 people for a city of 1 million inhabitants.

Can you imagine what this research means for your relationships at home, at work and your life in general?

If we learn not to judge others as well as ourselves and only concentrate on positive feelings such as peace, compassion, love and gratitude and the outcome we really wish with all our heart, change on infinite levels may occur.

Researchers then calculated the number of people it would take to create peace on Earth, and once again, the small number will astonish you:

It only needs 7746 of us for the 6 billion inhabitants of our Earth.

That's the power of your heart. That's the power of your mind. And that's the power of what you send out and why your inner message counts.

Final Words

May those results and stories give you hope. May they inspire you for your relationships, your work, your life and the World.

Clarity, focus and coherence are success tools that help to make your dreams come true. So, go inwards. Be very clear about what you expect and what you really want, adjust your inner message accordingly, and don't forget to imagine the best.

I wish you luck with these powerful tools. You have the power in you. If, however, you wish for intuitive reading or coaching, need help of any sort or want to know more about how to make your intuition work, please reach out. I am there for you.

Hunyah Irfan

HunyahTravels
Content Creator

https://www.linkedin.com/in/hunyah-irfan-blogger351/
https://www.facebook.com/OfficialHunyahTravels
https://www.instagram.com/officalhunyahtravels/
https://ca.linkedin.com/in/hunyah-irfan-blogger351

Hunyah is a content creator with a background in community development. You can find Hunyah doing food reviews, interviewing people and more. Hunyah is actively involved in the community for different events.

Empower Her Anthology: Breaking Stereotypes about the South Asian Community

By Hunyah Irfan

Hi, My name is Hunyah Irfan. I reside in Brampton, Ontario. Being brought up in a multicultural environment, I will be discussing breaking stereotypes about the South Asian community.

This is about perceptions of the South Asian community. Also, how stereotypes have evolved over the years, but there is a lot of progress at the same time.

These are the topics which I'm going to talk to you about :

1. Restaurants, Modern and Traditional
2. Shopping areas
3. Facilities
4. Community
5. Education
6. Dressing
7. Individualistic vs Collective mentality

Restaurants, Modern and Traditional

Being a South Asian food blogger, when you hear South Asian restaurants, you might think I'm referring to traditional food. For example, chicken tikka or red lentil meals.

In the early 2000s, when I was a kid, there weren't a lot of South Asian restaurants at the time. It used to be very limited to eat out at the time.

For example, South Asian-owned stakehouses weren't available at the time.

Now in Ontario, I'm talking about 2025, there are a lot of South Asian restaurants. But traditional food is like if you want to take out.

Modern South Asian restaurants have been trending a lot. Some of the South Asian recipes that are now having a new look to the traditional meals are from social media.

I'm not sure how many of these restaurants are owned by women, but these takes on social media for traditional South Asian recipes are from women.

That is innovative and invites everyone to try modern South Asian cuisine.

For example, chicken board to be served on occasion.

That is one way to break stereotypes.

But when it comes to stereotypes you have to know not everything is about your appearance. For myself I find out to be what you eat.

Nothing is wrong with eating, just the approach to what is South Asian food.

There are tons of influencers who are bringing new takes on South Asian food.

As a food blogger, I think this is progress and fusion cuisine.

Shopping Areas

Years ago in Canada, there weren't a lot of ethnic wear stores.

Now in 2025, every mall you go to, there is ethnic wear sold.

That is not just for South Asian wear but also for other ethnicities.

This is a good way of implementing ethnic wear into mainstream malls.

It's also breaking stereotypes of South Asian dressing as well.

Facilities

Where I live, recently, there has been new work of south asian long term in development.

Many years ago, facilities were limited for the South Asian community.

Now, mostly women are operating South Asian facilities.

This is like anything from clothes to long-term homes.

This has made a shift in terms of facilities.

I'm not sure exact what types of facilities but there is a lot in there.

This is a another way of breaking the stereotypes.

Communities

There is a huge South Asian community where I have lived since I was a kid.

With a number of South Asians living here, there is a huge change in terms of local events.

This from Diwali to Eid events.

That means exhibitions every month.

Plus, new businesses happening every year.

This is a huge global shift in women's success.

As the communities and people come to the events, more businesses are promoted, and people network.

These are my reasons why South Asian women are breaking stereotypes in the community.

Education

There is often stereotype of south asian women being not educated enough. That is not true.

Majority of the top women in different entrepreneurial journeys are south asian. There is a no limit to education. For example Manjit Minhas is one of the top south asian women entrepreneur right now. Then there is CEO of Anokhi magazine who interviews celebrities.

South Asian women are often underestimated for the education. There is stereotypes then you just turn 20 and get married. But that is not true all the time. Not the story every south asian women has. Yes, There is a milestones in life but most of the top South Asians are actually women.

Top Pakistani women is actually a actress who just won her first oscars which is recent news for the Pakistani community.

The debatable question is that should all women go into stereotypical careers for south asian or going into arts?

For myself, As artist being South Asian there is stereotypes.

That only being artist doesn't get you anywhere. That is a yes and no.

It is a good to be a artist but you work project to project. No you still a something in hand. Being an artist doesn't meet all your needs.

Dressing

Not all South Asian women are in traditional wear all the time. It depends on event and situation.

With me I'm most in pants on regular days. Usually traditional clothes are more for the events for example birthday, wedding and seasonal gathering.

Individualistic vs Collective mentality

In South Asian culture, Collective mentality is followed in many south asian families. That is really the family making the decisions for the person. I have seen this in my own family as well where some of the cousins have the whole family make the decisions for them.

How I grew up different from my own cousins? Is that I'm brought up with individualistic mentality. For myself I make decisions for me. I don't have the whole family decide for me what do I do in my life or not. For advice yes when I need to. But not for somethings. The somethings can be listed as clothes, career and gearing towards being independent.

When it comes to my cousins its not being so much independent. They don't think forward and still in time somewhere years back.

For me, I think forward and I think what is next to do.

Collective mentality is normal for most south asians but it is hard to be independent coming from collective mentality.

I don't know the exact number of how many south asians think like this. But its very normal. But individualistic mentality is still something new today for many south asians.

This also depends on eastern and western approach around the world as well.

Not just for Pakistanis but for Middle Eastern or African parts of the world. That is how decision making is taken.

This is my approach to breaking stereotypes on south asian being independent.

DK Hillard

Founder of DK Hillard Art, LLC
Artist/Designer/Author

https://www.linkedin.com/in/debra-hillard-93526913/
https://www.facebook.com/dkhillardart/
https://www.instagram.com/dkhillard/
https://www.dkhillardart.com/

Debra is a creator. It is how she lives and what she does in her work. Her art has been a consistent thread throughout her life, whether it be painting, writing or working with others. It is based in her spiritual journey, her Shamanic practice and her connection to nature. For 20 years she was a life coach and personal trainer, a career that evolved out of her experience transforming her life through bodybuilding. During that time she developed a 12 week program using the body as a vehicle for transforming your entire life. She transforms her paintings into sensual, luxurious fabrics- clothing, blankets and pillows called "Wraptures", bringing the energy of her artwork into forms you can touch. They are filled with the love that she puts into everything she creates. She works with individuals and small groups using many of the interactive processes she developed while teaching her program.

Awakening the Divine: Embracing the Global Shift of Women's Sacred Power and Worth

By DK Hillard

It was a time of war. Plagues ravaged the earth, and death hung in the air.

I lived in a village where the sun seldom shone through the thick clouds. My mind was a vast garden of wisdom, and my heart a compass that could navigate the most treacherous of storms. I was gifted with an intuition so sharp that I could hear the whispers of the wind, read the movements of the stars, and feel the pulse of the earth beneath my feet. But in a time when the shadows of patriarchy stretched long, such gifts were feared, for they were seen as dangerous, uncontainable, and defiant.

I learned early to conceal my brilliance. My knowledge was my secret, buried deep beneath the quiet hum of daily life. I tended to my family with grace, spoke only when spoken to, and dressed my words in modesty. Beneath my hands, the herbs I grew seemed to bloom with an intelligence of their own, and my silences carried more weight than many of the loudest voices. But I kept my gifts hidden, for I knew that to reveal them would lead to peril.

The village, ruled by men who believed in the strength of their own power, demanded that women stay in their place—silent, obedient, unseen. The whispers of women with gifts, with knowledge, or with a spark of fire in their hearts were swiftly silenced by fear of retribution. I had witnessed firsthand the deadly consequences of speaking my truth—of being seen for who I truly was.

One day, a great drought struck the land. The crops withered, the rivers ran dry, and despair spread like wildfire. Violence erupted, the men using it as an excuse to plunder and pillage. Yet, as the days passed and the land grew more barren, my intuition became a voice I could no longer ignore. I stood as if from another time and place, witnessing the village under siege.

Buildings in flames, women screaming with the violent violation of their bodies, villagers running for their lives. There was no color anywhere, just grey death. Beside me, witnessing the destruction, were two fellow priestesses, witches with another name. Our powers combined would bring this devastation to a halt if we so chose.

The village men gathered in the council, searching for a solution, but their minds could not pierce the darkness of the problem. They debated endlessly, their voices raised in confusion, but no answers came. The men looked only at the surface of the issue and could not see beyond their own eyes.

We three stepped into the clearing, where the men were gathered in frustration, and offered a quiet suggestion: "Perhaps the answer lies not in your efforts, but in listening to the land. Perhaps the roots, deep beneath the earth, hold the wisdom we need."

The men scoffed, not understanding our words, and continued their deliberations. To them, we were almost invisible. In a quiet act of defiance, I called upon unseen forces, bringing the two other women to my side. With a whispered chant, we summoned the forces of the earth and the winds, asking for guidance, trusting in the knowledge we had long kept hidden.

Among us, a current of energy surged, an ancient wisdom and magic shared as sisters. No one noticed us, for we were invisible to most, sent to heal and bring life to a broken world. Joining hands and blending minds, we activated all the power within us and watched as the flames that had raged only moments before were extinguished. To the astonishment of all, the waters began to rise. Slowly, a hidden spring deep within the earth was awakened. The screaming turned to laughter, and the cold, grey death that had blanketed the village, bloomed with spring flowers. Children returned to their play, and animals roamed the village. I could smell the familiar aroma of bread baking and the earth coming back to life beneath our feet. A feeling of peace seemed to float among the homes, now vibrant with hope and love. All memories of war disappeared. We knew that our work was done, the healing powers within us were used for good, and it was time to move on. But the men, too proud to acknowledge the women who had saved them, claimed the discovery as their own.

I, knowing the truth, returned to my quiet life. My gifts were once again hidden, but now, they were more powerful than ever. Though the world would not see my brilliance, it could no longer silence it.

The lesson passed down through the ages for all women of power: True power is not in the loudness of one's voice or the fear of what others may do. It lies in the quiet strength to listen, to trust one's gifts, and to know when the time is right to let them shine—no matter the cost.

* * *

I have had these visions most of my life. In my youth, they frightened me, but as my spiritual practice deepened, I leaned into my truth with more courage and resolve to use the gifts I had been given.

Who I am and what I am here for is clear. I came back to claim my truth and walk through the world as who I am without shame, apology, or fear. I came to offer whatever gifts I have, to bring color back to the world and love to our hearts.

I ran from the truth because of the persecution I suffered at others' hands so many times over. My powers were misunderstood, which made them a threat to others and a danger to myself. This is a theme running through multiple lifetimes, as a warrior, a witch, a shaman, and a priestess. I came back to claim my truth and embody it, to use it in the ways it was intended and walk through the world as who I truly am. But I am not alone in this. Women all over the globe are remembering and rising to effect change.

* * *

My mother was a brilliant, intuitive woman, born in a time when none of that was appreciated. The eldest of three sisters, she found herself tasked with setting an example she didn't care to set. My mother's dreams were larger than she was allowed, and in her own small way, she rebelled against the tyranny of her parent's expectations. Not unlike the time of the three priestesses, my mother's time was not safe for women to excel, especially in areas such as intuition. Her voice was silenced, but her desires still burned.

She was taught to marry well, and what that entailed did not fit the man she fell in love with, so she went against her parents' wishes, and we all paid the price of their wrath. I was born into a family where resentment ran deep, judgment and condemnation for being true to yourself, a given and any truth was silenced. Over and over again, I was told that I did not feel what I felt, think what I thought, or want anything that was acceptable. I, myself, was unacceptable just for being me. Like my mother before me, I had gifts, a keen mind and a sense of things that others did not. But my mother found herself both resentful and afraid of me, perhaps for being brash enough to state the obvious and audacious enough to insist on being myself.

I grew up in a time when our culture was in an uproar. All norms were being challenged. But women were still under men's thumb. Somewhere deep within me, I remembered who I was—the third Priestess/Witch whose power for good could heal the world. I dared not speak it, though. Times were changing, but it was still too soon for the truth to be told.

I watched my brilliant mother wither under my father's judgment and patriarchal power. I listened as he told me to shush my own thoughts in favor of keeping the peace with my family. Even when he knew I spoke the truth, he wouldn't allow it to interfere with the status quo of our quietly abusive family unit. Both my parents had grown up with abuse, and my experience was no different. Just like patriarchal views are passed down from generation to generation, so are patterns that perpetuate abusive behavior. Ours was a quiet form of it all. Perhaps my father's disappointment over me being born female was part of it, or maybe it was that I scared both my parents so much. I was different and not easily hushed. However, the patterns became part of my DNA, and it would take a lifetime to break them.

Over the course of my lifetime, I watched as my mother's voice began to disappear. She rarely expressed herself, but as the years passed, I found myself having to listen ever more closely to actually hear the words coming from her mouth. It was as if she was swallowing the words instead of releasing them. She was disappearing into herself, down a hole that eventually led to her death. It was only for a brief few years after my father's passing that she started to show her true colors. Not all of it was pleasant. There was both a sadness and an anger bubbling up now that the weight of his power over her was gone. For a long time, I blamed myself for the loss in her life. If only she hadn't had me, maybe she would have been able to pursue her dreams. She blamed me for a while, outwardly telling me how much she wished she had had a different life. But underneath it all, I suspect she knew the truth. At least towards the end, when she and I came to a place of peace and resolution with the events of our past.

My mother lived in spoonfuls, never taking life by the reins and making it her own. As determined as I was not to do the same, I found myself in an abusive marriage, not unlike the one my mother had endured. It took me almost thirty years to get out, see the truth, and be willing to save my own life. But that was a time when the winds of change had already taken hold, and women were beginning to stand their ground. My sister, ten years my senior, had not had the benefit of those changing times. She was caught in the middle between her dreams and a world where being a mother and wife was most important. Brilliant, creative, and powerful, my sister still fights the good fight but was not able to completely break free of the patterns that lived in our DNA, the patterns that took hold of so many women over the years.

Part of the shift I see in women comes from something my mother could not fathom. In her generation and for many before her, women were not taught to receive. Women were the givers, the selfless mothers, daughters, wives. The ones who sacrificed everything for their family's happiness. They were the women who stood in the background while their husbands received all the praise, asking only for leftover crumbs. I saw it in my family. My mother, the smart one, the one who had the answer before the question was ever asked, and the one who didn't speak it so that my father wouldn't feel like less. She faded into the background like a good wife and mother should, teaching both my sister and me what a "good" woman did. I was angry back then, infuriated that she would work all day and cook at night with no help from my father. He sat with his paper while she cleaned up the mess and then went to turn on the TV as she started the laundry. When I spoke up, he scolded me, and she cowered. I was angry and rebellious, but the effect on my DNA was powerful. It took me many decades to relearn my own worth and just as many to learn to receive with grace.

As I've learned to receive, I've discovered that it creates space for deeper connection and growth. The more I open myself to what others offer, the more I see the beauty of life's reciprocity. When you allow yourself to receive, you honor not only the giver but also the life you're living—the full spectrum of experiences, lessons, and love that it brings. It's a practice of humility and grace, one that invites a richer, more balanced existence.

Now, my passion flows because I am learning to allow abundance to enter, to nourish me as I nourish others. I savor the friendships I've cultivated, find joy in creating a home filled with meaning, and celebrate the beauty that arises from each act of creation. I welcome the appreciation I receive for the wisdom I share, knowing it is a reflection of the love and grace I have allowed into my life.

I see a growing shift in women's embrace of their own value, and a bold willingness to receive the compensation and the praise they truly deserve. That is not hubris. It is self-love and self-respect. When women can gracefully receive their due, the scales will begin to balance, and I believe this time is coming.

* * *

We are in the throes of much change in the world. It is a time of great upheaval, and my sense is that women are the key to whether we survive as a species or not. The patriarchy, though still strong, is weakening in its overreaching power, and women are rising to speak the truth and make change. Men of the younger generations are more aware and less tolerant of the old ways. They are more prone to see women as their equals and turn to them for their strengths. This shift is about men as well as women because it requires all of us to shift the patterns of generations.

In recent years, the world has witnessed a profound shift in the way we define and experience success, particularly for women. This shift is not just a passing trend or a surface-level change; it's a fundamental transformation in how we see ourselves, how we live, and what we stand for. It's a revolution, not in the conventional sense of taking power through political structures or institutions, but a quiet yet unstoppable wave of awakening in women everywhere—an awakening to their own inherent power, creativity, and wisdom.

From the viewpoint of my own creative and shamanic work, this shift is nothing short of revolutionary. As a visionary and artist, I have watched firsthand as women have begun to reclaim their true essence—no longer confined to outdated roles or expectations, but embracing their authentic selves, their inherent creativity, and their spiritual calling. This new era of women's success is not about fitting into the traditional framework of achievement defined by external markers such as wealth, status, or traditional careers. Instead, it is about tapping into something deeper, more personal, and more spiritual. This is a shift toward success rooted in authenticity, inner wisdom, and creative expression. It's a shift that calls for healing, transformation, and a deep connection to the Earth and the self.

I see it also in changing views on aging, especially in women across the globe. Myself, a woman in her older years, feared aging as a curse to those who had dreams and made their mark. In my mother's world, a woman of my age was already dismissed and invisible. Now, I look back at who she was and what she could have offered if given the opportunity and I know that women of my generation and younger will not allow that to happen again. We are reclaiming our potency, and aging has become a sign of having lived, experienced, and accumulated enough wisdom to be of great value. Other cultures have realized this long before we did, honoring their elders and using their wisdom for guidance and counsel.

The creative visionaries leading the way in this movement are women who refuse to be confined by the structures that once dictated their lives. They are women who know that the world needs a new kind of leadership—one rooted in creativity, intuition, and heart-centered action. These women, many of whom are artists, spiritual leaders, and entrepreneurs, are redefining what it means to be successful. And they are doing so by leaning into their unique gifts, their creativity, and their inner knowing, undeterred by those who attempt to mute their voices.

In my own journey as a creative visionary, I have seen how success is no longer just about external validation or meeting the expectations of others. For many women today, success is about stepping into their creative power and using their art and intuition as tools for personal transformation and collective change. It is about following the path that resonates with their soul's calling, rather than the one that conforms to societal pressures.

Art, for me, is more than just a form of expression; it is a channel through which I can connect to the divine and bring healing, clarity, and empowerment to others. As women tap into their creativity, they are stepping into their power in ways that are both personal and global. The act of creation itself becomes an act of liberation—a reclaiming of the self and an offering to the world. Every painting, every piece of writing, every piece of music or performance becomes a prayer, a reflection of one's deepest truths, and a tool for transformation. Women are no longer seeking to create for the approval of others but are creating to express the fullness of their being and to contribute to a collective healing.

This creative awakening is at the heart of the global shift in women's success. The more women embrace their creative potential, the more they empower themselves to live authentically. This is not just about artistic careers or fame; it's about using creativity as a means of healing and empowerment. It's about turning inward, listening to one's intuition, and allowing that inner wisdom to guide one's path—whether that's through art, business, activism, or any other form of self-expression. The global shift in women's success is, at its core, about creating a new paradigm of leadership—one that is rooted in authenticity, emotional intelligence, and the courage to be vulnerable. Women know at our core that vulnerability is a strength. We know that true power does not lie in force, dominance, or victory, but in humility, unity, and the strength of character to uplift others.

As I have integrated my own shamanic practices into my work, I have witnessed how spirituality and deep inner wisdom are also playing an integral role in the global shift toward women's success. Shamanism, with its emphasis on connection to the Earth, ancestral knowledge, and the unseen forces that guide us, has become a powerful tool for women seeking to reclaim their power. Through shamanic practices, women are rediscovering the strength of their intuitive abilities, the wisdom of their bodies, and the sacredness of their connection to the land.

The rise of shamanic practices among women is not just a trend—it is a reclamation of ancient knowledge that has long been suppressed by patriarchal systems. For centuries, women's connection to spirituality, the Earth, and their own intuition was deemed dangerous, unruly, and subversive. But today, more and more women are remembering the power of their innate connection to the Earth and the spirit world. This reclamation of shamanic wisdom is one of the cornerstones of the shift we are seeing in women's success.

Through practices like shamanism, women are learning to heal themselves, connect with their ancestors, and access the sacred wisdom that has been passed down through generations. They are reconnecting with their bodies, their emotions, and their deep knowing. This connection to spiritual wisdom allows women to navigate the world in a way that is authentic, grounded, and aligned with their purpose.

For many women, shamanic practices offer a path to healing and empowerment. Whether it is through journeying, ritual, or working with plant medicine, these practices provide a means of accessing deep wisdom and understanding that transcends the limitations of the mind. Women are learning to trust their intuition, listen to the messages of their bodies, and trust the cycles of nature as a guide for their personal and professional lives. Shamanism teaches women how to trust their own inner guidance, how to navigate the challenges of life with grace, and how to heal from the wounds that have been passed down through generations.

This spiritual awakening is a critical part of the global shift toward women's success because when women are more fully in their power, the world around them heals. As women reconnect with their spiritual power and their ancestral wisdom, they are tapping into an energy that transcends the limitations of the modern world. They are embracing their role as leaders, healers, and creators in ways that are grounded in a deep connection to the Earth and the unseen realms. This spiritual empowerment is a key element of the new era of women's success, where success is not measured by external accolades but by an internal sense of alignment and purpose.

Art has always been a powerful tool for transformation, but in the context of this global shift, it has taken on an even deeper significance. Women today are using art as a way to express their innermost truths, heal old wounds, and catalyze societal change. Through their art, they are reclaiming their voices, their bodies, and their power. Art becomes a form of resistance against the forces that seek to silence or marginalize women. It becomes a vehicle for healing—both for the individual and for the collective.

In my own work, I have seen how art can be a deeply transformative tool. It can help women process trauma, navigate their emotions, and connect to a higher sense of purpose. I use it as a tool to help women (and men) remember their truth and activate it in their everyday lives. Art, especially forms that engage physical senses beyond eyesight, can bypass the conscious mind and help you connect deeply with long-buried truths. I use my work in this way, combining my artistry with my spiritual practice and the uniquely feminine intuitive sense I have developed over the decades.

But art is also a way of connecting to the collective consciousness. As more women create art that is rooted in their own truth and experiences, they are contributing to a collective healing that is rippling out across the globe.

This is the power of art in the new era of women's success. Women are no longer creating to fit into existing molds or to please external authorities—they are creating to express their own inner truths, to heal, and to contribute to the collective good. The act of creating becomes an act of self-love and self-empowerment, and in doing so, it becomes a way of contributing to the healing of the world.

At the heart of the global shift in women's success is a redefinition of leadership. The rise of women in the arts, entrepreneurship, and spiritual practices is bringing forth a new form of leadership—one that is not about hierarchy, power, or dominance but about collaboration, compassion, and emotional intelligence. Women are stepping into leadership roles in a way that is aligned with their values, their intuition, and their connection to the Earth.

This new form of leadership is not about competition—it's about collaboration. Women are coming together, supporting one another, and lifting each other up. The success of one woman becomes the success of all, and together, they are creating a new world—a world that is more inclusive, more compassionate, and more attuned to the needs of the planet.

The global shift in women's success is not just about personal achievement—it is about collective transformation. It is about creating a world where women are empowered to live their truth, to express their creativity, and to contribute to the healing of the world. Through their art, their spirituality, and their leadership, women are showing the world what true success looks like: success that is rooted in authenticity, collaboration, and love.

Women all over the world are waking up to their own power and potential, and they are stepping into their roles as leaders, healers, and creators. This is a movement that is unstoppable, one that is rooted in creativity, intuition, and love. And as more women embrace their authentic selves and their creative power, they will continue to transform the world, creating a future that is more connected, more compassionate, and more aligned with the needs of the Earth.

My work as a priestess, guide, and creative visionary is rooted in one core principle: to walk my own truth. By living authentically, I create the space for others to do the same. This is a responsibility we all share—to embrace our truth and use our unique gifts for the collective good. For many years, I was told that my creative abilities were unimportant, that they were not valued or desired. But over time, I've come to realize that these very gifts are exactly what I was meant to offer in service to the world, especially as we undergo this profound global shift.

As an artist, my ability to sense, feel, and perceive deeply—beyond the visible, into the unseen world—has become my strength. I bring forth treasures from these realms, translating them into creations that help others connect with their own inner truths. This process is deeply spiritual; it's a sacred act of remembrance. It has taken me a lifetime to fully own these gifts and to recognize them not as anomalies but as essential tools that I was meant to use in this time of transformation.

Raised in an era when such intuitive abilities were often dismissed or misunderstood, I now see that things are shifting. The world is waking up to the value of these gifts, and more and more people are embracing their own unique abilities. Through my art, my guidance, and my priestess's work, I offer a space where these gifts can be nurtured, seen, and celebrated.

My offerings are an invitation for you to reconnect with your own deeper knowing, to unlock the potential within you, and to bring your own gifts into the world for the healing and transformation of all. Whether through creative expression, spiritual guidance, or transformative experiences, I am here to walk with you as you discover and embrace your truest self.

Feeling inspired by what you've just read and ready to explore further? I offer a transformative process to help you reconnect with the truth of who you are, creating unique and powerful anchors through my art. Reach out to me here to start your journey.

JOIN THE MOVEMENT!
#BAUW

Becoming An Unstoppable Woman
With She Rises Studios

She Rises Studios was founded by Hanna Olivas and Adriana Luna Carlos, the mother-daughter duo, in mid-2020 as they saw a need to help empower women worldwide. They are the podcast hosts of the *She Rises Studios Podcast* and Amazon best-selling authors and motivational speakers who travel the world. Hanna and Adriana are the movement creators of #BAUW - Becoming An Unstoppable Woman: The movement has been created to universally impact women of all ages, at whatever stage of life, to overcome insecurities, and adversities, and develop an unstoppable mindset. She Rises Studios educates, celebrates, and empowers women globally.

Looking to Join Us in our Next Anthology or Publish YOUR Own?

She Rises Studios Publishing offers full-service publishing, marketing, book tour, and campaign services. For more information, contact info@sherisesstudios.com

We are always looking for women who want to share their stories and expertise and feature their businesses on our podcasts, in our books, and in our magazines.

SEE WHAT WE DO

OUR PODCAST	OUR BOOKS	OUR SERVICES

Be featured in the Becoming An Unstoppable Woman magazine, published in 13 countries and sold in all major retailers. Get the visibility you need to LEVEL UP in your business!

Have your own TV show streamed across major platforms like Roku TV, Amazon Fire Stick, Apple TV and more!

Learn to leverage your expertise. Build your online presence and grow your audience with FENIX TV.
https://fenixtv.sherisesstudios.com/

Visit www.SheRisesStudios.com to see how YOU can join the #BAUW movement and help your community to achieve the UNSTOPPABLE mindset.

Have you checked out the *She Rises Studios Podcast?*

Find us on all MAJOR platforms: Spotify, IHeartRadio, Apple Podcasts, Google Podcasts, etc.

Looking to become a sponsor or build a partnership?

Email us at info@sherisesstudios.com

www.ingramcontent.com/pod-product-compliance
Lightning Source LLC
Chambersburg PA
CBHW071102120626
46546CB00003B/1253